The Black Archive #13

HUMAN NATURE / THE FAMILY OF BLOOD

By Naomi Jacobs and
Philip Purser-Hallard

Also Available

The Black Archive #1: Rose by Jon Arnold
The Black Archive #2: The Massacre by James Cooray Smith
The Black Archive #3: The Ambassadors of Death by LM Myles
The Black Archive #4: Dark Water / Death in Heaven by Philip Purser-Hallard
The Black Archive #5: Image of the Fendahl by Simon Bucher-Jones
The Black Archive #6: Ghost Light by Jonathan Dennis
The Black Archive #7: The Mind Robber by Andrew Hickey
The Black Archive #8: Black Orchid by Ian Millsted
The Black Archive #9: The God Complex by Paul Driscoll
The Black Archive #10: Scream of the Shalka by Jon Arnold
The Black Archive #11: The Evil of the Daleks by Simon Guerrier
The Black Archive #12: Pyramids of Mars by Kate Orman

Coming Soon

The Black Archive #14: The Ultimate Foe by James Cooray Smith
The Black Archive #15: Carnival of Monsters by Ian Potter
The Black Archive #16: The Twin Dilemma by Gordon Ridout
The Black Archive #17: Full Circle by John Toon
The Black Archive #18: Marco Polo by Dene October
The Black Archive #19: The Impossible Planet / The Satan Pit by Simon Bucher-Jones
The Black Archive #20: Face the Raven by Sarah Groenewegen
The Black Archive #21: Heaven Sent by Kara Dennison
The Black Archive #22: Hell Bent by Alyssa Franke
The Black Archive #23: The Curse of Fenric by Una McCormack
The Black Archive #24: The Time Warrior by Matthew Kilburn
The Black Archive #25: Doctor Who (1996) by Paul Driscoll
The Black Archive #26: The Dæmons by Matt Barber

Published September 2017 by Obverse Books
Cover Design © Cody Schell

Range editor: Philip Purser-Hallard

Naomi and Philip would like to thank:

Sunday Swift for consultation on Chapter 2, and James Cooray Smith and Stuart Douglas for editing assistance

CONTENTS

OVERVIEW

Serial Title: *Human Nature / The Family of Blood*

Writer: Paul Cornell

Director: Charles Palmer

Original UK Transmission Dates: 26 May – 2 June 2007

Running Time: *Human Nature*: 45m 1s

The Family of Blood 42m 59s

UK Viewing Figures: *Human Nature*: 7.7 million

The Family of Blood 7.2 million

Regular cast: David Tennant (The Doctor / Smith[1]), Freema Agyeman (Martha)

Guest Cast: Jessica Hynes (Joan Redfern), Rebekah Staton (Jenny), Thomas Sangster (Tim Latimer), Harry Lloyd (Baines), Tom Palmer (Hutchinson), Gerard Horan (Clark), Lauren Wilson (Lucy Cartwright), Pip Torrens (Rocastle), Matthew White (Phillips), Derek Smith (Doorman), Peter Bourke (Mr Chambers), Sophie Turner (Vicar)

Antagonists: The Family of Blood

Adapted from: *Human Nature* by Paul Cornell. **Doctor Who: The New Adventures**.

---

[1] Credited as 'The Doctor / Smith' in *Human Nature*, and 'The Doctor' in *The Family of Blood*.

Responses:

'I consider the TV rendition of *Human Nature* to be a half-decent cover version; it's more along the lines of Johnny Cash covering "One" than Boyzone murdering "Father and Son". Still, it's not Jimi Hendrix doing "All Along The Watchtower" either.'

[Mike Morris, 'Adapt to Survive', *The Doctor Who Ratings Guide*]

'[T]he most fun I've had in front of the TV for years.'

[Ben Aaronovitch, comment on Paul Cornell's blog ('The Family of Blood')]

SYNOPSIS

Human Nature

John Smith, a history teacher at an English boys' boarding school in 1913, dreams of being **the Doctor**, a time-travelling adventurer from another world. The matron at the school, **Joan Redfern**, and **Martha Jones**, his servant, reassure him that he is thoroughly human.

When a bright light appears in the night sky, Smith dismisses it as a distant meteorite. However, during an illicit night-time excursion an older boy named **Baines** discovers an invisible spaceship, and is abducted by its disembodied occupants, **the Family**. Disturbed by the sighting, Martha visits the Doctor's hidden 'magic box', the TARDIS, and remembers her friend's decision to become human. It is a temporary measure intended to avoid the Family, who are vicious but short-lived predators, tracking his scent across time and space. The TARDIS has created an entire false history for him as Smith, while his Time Lord nature is backed up in a pocket-watch.

This watch fascinates **Tim Latimer**, a younger boy with a psychic aptitude for accurate guesses, and while visiting Smith's rooms he appropriates it. One of the Family, who has returned to the school in Baines' form, detects its Time Lord scent and mobilises an army of **scarecrows** to choose local bodies for the rest of his Family: they select a farmer called **Mr Clark**, a young girl named **Lucy Cartwright**, and Martha's fellow maid **Jenny**.

A vision of the coming First World War distracts Tim during cadet training, and Smith gives an older boy, **Hutchinson**, permission to beat him. On a walk to the nearby village, Joan tells Smith that the cadets remind her of her husband's death in the Boer War. Smith demonstrates a surprising non-military heroism by saving a baby's life with a cricket ball, and the superhumanly lucky trick emboldens him to ask Joan to a dance at the village hall. Seeing them together, Martha realises that the Doctor left her no instructions on what to do if Smith fell in love.

The false Jenny's bizarre behaviour alerts Martha to the Family's presence. Unable to find the pocket-watch, she nevertheless insists that it is time for Smith to become the Doctor again. Embarrassed by her behaviour in front of Joan, he sacks her, but she turns up at the village dance with the sonic screwdriver from his dreams. The false Lucy overhears their conversation and learns the truth about Smith.

The Family and their scarecrows gatecrash the dance. They threaten to kill Martha and Joan, demanding that the baffled Smith change himself back into a Time Lord.

The Family of Blood

As Smith dithers, Martha takes charge of the situation and holds the false 'Jenny' hostage while the dance guests make their escape. She, Smith and Joan return to the school, which is soon besieged by the Family. 'Baines' kills a teacher, **Mr Phillips**, and demands that the headmaster, **Mr Rocastle**, hand Smith over. Rocastle, a Boer War veteran, puts his cadets on a war footing to defend the school. Smith tries, but finds himself unable, to fire a gun against the invaders.

After experiencing his wartime vision again, Tim deserts his position and runs into 'Lucy'. He uses the pocket-watch to repel her, but gives away its significance. The Family attack: Rocastle is killed and Hutchinson is traumatised at the reality of combat. Eventually Smith, the women and the boys retreat, but not before the Family show Smith that they have the TARDIS.

By now Joan has come to believe Martha's story, but Smith remains in denial. The three take refuge at the house of the murdered Cartwright family. Soon the hunters return to their spaceship and begin bombarding the village. When Tim arrives with the watch, Smith is faced with a terrible dilemma. If he does nothing, the Family will destroy the villagers. If he hands over the watch, they will use the Doctor's essence to become immortal. If he opens the watch, Smith will die, replaced by a being so inhuman that the prospect of falling in love never occurred to him.

After the watch shows him and Joan a vision of their possible future together, Smith makes his choice. He goes to the Family's spaceship and surrenders the watch to them. They find that it is empty.

In fact 'Smith' is now the Doctor, and this brief distraction is all the restored Time Lord needs to sabotage and blow up their ship. He inflicts baroque eternal punishments on the members of the Family, granting them their longed-for immortality. The creature posing as Baines comes to realise that, in merely avoiding them until they died, the Doctor had hoped to show them mercy.

The Doctor offers the bereaved Joan a life aboard the TARDIS, which she refuses. He and Martha say goodbye to Tim, who, prompted by his vision, goes on to save Hutchinson's life during the War. A lifetime later, as a very old man, Tim sees the time-travellers again at a Remembrance Day service.

NOTES ON TERMINOLOGY

Of necessity, this book refers often to both the two-part 2007 **Doctor Who** TV story *Human Nature / The Family of Blood* which is its primary focus, and to the 1995 **Doctor Who: The New Adventures** novel *Human Nature* from which the story was adapted.

To avoid ambiguity, in this study:

- '*Human Nature* [NA]' is used to refer to the novel, in any of its various editions.
- '*Human Nature* [TV]' refers solely to the first episode of the two-part TV story, and '*The Family of Blood*' to the second episode alone.
- '*Human Nature / The Family of Blood*' refers to the two-parter as a whole.

The novel itself has been through several editions (see the Bibliography for further details):

- The original, published in 1995 as part of Virgin Publishing's **New Adventures** series ('1995 ed').
- The online ebook version added to the BBC **Doctor Who** website in 2002 ('ebook'). In June 2007 additional notes by Paul Cornell on 'Adapting the Novel for the Screen' were added. The ebook is no longer available on the BBC site, but can be found on the Wayback Machine Internet Archive.
- The reissued paperback edition, published by BBC Books in 2015 as part of the eight-book **History**

Collection ('2015 ed'). An electronic version for ebook readers was issued concurrently.

For convenience, except where otherwise noted, page references to *Human Nature* [NA] in this study will be to the currently most widely available version, the 2015 reissue. Minor textual differences between the editions will be noted where relevant. References to 'ebook' (mostly to the notes and other additional material) are to the web version, **not** to the electronic counterpart of the 2015 paperback. They use the pagination in the PDF file, as updated in 2007.

Finally, the alien antagonists in *Human Nature / The Family of Blood* are given no names, referring to themselves only by their family relationships ('Mother-of-Mine' and the like). They are identified in the credits by the names of the individuals whose identities they adopt: Jenny, Baines, Lucy Cartwright and Mr Clark. We refer to the alien replicas by these names, but use quote marks to distinguish them from the originals, their victims. Thus, it is Baines who leaves the school to find beer in *Human Nature* [TV], but 'Baines' who returns in his place.

INTRODUCTION

The Black Archive does not deal with **Doctor Who** in media other than television. This is not because these other media are qualitatively inferior or thematically less interesting – any impartial observer will be able to discover many cases where the reverse is true. Nor is it simply because **Doctor Who** was created for the TV medium and remains most at home there, the anchor to which all tie-in media are tied.

It is, in fact, simply because the TV series is the most popular form of **Doctor Who**. Thousands of people, perhaps even tens of thousands, may have read Paul Cornell's **Doctor Who** comic strip *The Chameleon Factor* (1991) or his **Doctor Who** novel *Happy Endings* (1996), or listened to his **Doctor Who** audio story *The Shadow of the Scourge* (2000). More than 8 million saw his first **Doctor Who** TV story, *Father's Day* (2005).

With the history of **Doctor Who** in its sixth decade, with dozens of separate publishers having produced **Doctor Who** in books, comics, audio stories, websites, computer games, role-playing games and other fictional formats; with spin-off media from many other publishers featuring the continuing exploits of the Doctor's associates from Colonel Lethbridge-Stewart to the Pharaoh Erimemushinteperem; with **Doctor Who**'s 21st-century revival having achieved such cultural penetration by 2017 that the 12th Doctor is an optional character in the *Lego Dimensions* PC game and the Daleks make an appearance in *The Lego Batman Movie*; who but the most assiduous (and, let us be honest, affluent) collector could possibly hope to amass, let alone actually experience, all the stories connected to the **Doctor Who** universe?

Yet nearly everyone who cares about the Doctor's adventures watches the TV series – or has in the past, even if any given current iteration happens not to be to their taste. Ultimately, a focus on the TV series is the best way for a series such as **The Black Archive** to ensure that it covers ground that will be common to most of its readers.

During the years between 1989 and 2005, though, there was no TV series. In 1991, with **Doctor Who** cancelled and absent from television, a range of licensed **Doctor Who** books was launched by Virgin Publishing which would run for five years, and produce 61 novels. These '**New Adventures**' formed a continuing narrative, following the seventh Doctor and various companions. By the mid-1990s, they were the only place to go to follow the Doctor's continuing adventures[2]. At the time of the **New Adventures**' publication, they were considered by many to be the primary continuation of the Doctor's story. Aside from the *Doctor Who Magazine* (DWM) comic strips (which followed **New Adventures** continuity until 1994 and did not diverge from it explicitly until

---

[2] Certainly this was the editorial intention: the Preface to the first **New Adventure** stated that the books would 'continue the time and space peregrinations of the Doctor and Ace from the point at which we last saw them on television, at the end of the story *Survival* (Darvill-Evans, Peter, 'Preface', Peel, Jon, *Timewyrm: Genesys*, front matter). Later, after the *Doctor Who Magazine* comic strip, the Big Finish audio plays and the 21st-century iteration of the TV series had taken **Doctor Who** in their own direction independent of the **New Adventures**, Cornell would note that 'In these days [...] of splintered canons, it's surprising to remember that back then we only had one universe, and everybody lived in it' (quoted in Guerrier, Simon, *Bernice Summerfield: The Inside Story*, p19).

1996), there were no other media. If a former **Doctor Who** viewer was interested in what the Doctor had been doing since *Survival* (1989), then like it or not – and many did not, just as there have always been many who have taken issue with the TV series, in any of its various iterations – the **New Adventures** were the only game in town.

One of the initial authors was Paul Cornell, who would write five novels for the range (together with the Virgin **Missing Adventures** novel *Goth Opera* (1994) and two related comic stories for DWM). The fourth of these, published in 1995, was the much-acclaimed *Human Nature* [NA][3]. A decade later the novel was reworked by Cornell into the two episodes of the 2007 series with David Tennant as the Doctor, *Human Nature* and *The Family of Blood*, which form the focus of this volume.

It is true that other episodes of the 21st-century series have been based on content in other media. *Blink*, the story which followed *The Family of Blood* in the 2007 season, began as an adaptation by Steven Moffat of his short story 'What I Did on My Christmas Holidays by Sally Sparrow' from the *Doctor Who Annual 2006* (2005)[4]. Rob Shearman's earlier episode *Dalek* (2005) was a reworking of some of the themes and concepts from his 2003

---

[3] *Human Nature* [NA] was voted 'Favourite **New Adventure**' of 1995 in *Doctor Who Magazine* (DWM)'s 1996 Reader Survey (Jackson, Elizabeth, 'The 1996 *Doctor Who Magazine* Survey Results', DWM #240), and 'Top **New Adventure**' out of the full range in the 35th anniversary 'DWM Awards' poll (Owen, Dave, 'The Best (and Worst) of Virgin', DWM #265).

[4] Also available on the BBC website, somewhat misleadingly titled 'Blink: The Original Story'.

Doctor Who audio drama *Jubilee*, published by Big Finish Productions, and the 2006 two-parter *Rise of the Cybermen / The Age of Steel* was even more tenuously based on the Big Finish audio drama *Spare Parts* (2002).

Cross-media propagation has happened in other contexts as well – not least in the novelisation of (to date) all but two 20th-century **Doctor Who** TV stories, but also for example in the 1960s **Dalek** films[5], the multiple versions of *Shada*[6] and Big Finish's range of audio adaptations of **Doctor Who** novels (mostly **New Adventures**), which began with Jacqueline Rayner's 2012 reworking of Cornell's own *Love and War* (1992). What makes *Human Nature* [NA] unique is that it is the only full-length **Doctor Who** novel adapted, by its original author no less, for television.

The overall influence of the Virgin books, and their BBC-published successors, on Russell T Davies' 21st-century revival of **Doctor Who** is difficult to gauge with accuracy. In addition to Cornell, Davies himself contributed to the **New Adventures** (though his novel, *Damaged Goods* (1996), is tonally very unlike the relaunched TV show[7]), as did Mark Gatiss, Matt Jones and Gareth Roberts, each of whom would write two episodes of the TV series during Davies's

---

[5] *Dr Who and the Daleks* (1965), an adaptation of *The Daleks* (1963-64), and *Daleks: Invasion Earth 2150 AD* (1966), which adapted *The Dalek Invasion of Earth* (1964). Both TV stories were also novelised.

[6] This partially-made story, scripted by Douglas Adams, went unbroadcast in 1980 but has since been: released on VHS (1992) and DVD (2013) in a version with linking narration by Tom Baker; adapted as an animated webcast starring Paul McGann which was also released without imagery as an audio CD (2003); and novelised by Gareth Roberts (2012).

[7] See Arnold, Jon, *The Black Archive #1: Rose* (2016), pp77-78.

tenure as showrunner[8]. In most cases it can be argued that the innovations of the 21st-century series – for example its greater emphasis on the characterisation and relationships of the companions, its explicit acknowledgement of sexuality, and its shift in the direction of long-form storytelling rather than isolated adventures – were the products of the changes in TV drama practice since 1989, and would have taken place regardless of whatever evolution **Doctor Who** in other media had undergone in the interim.

In the case of *Human Nature / The Family of Blood*, however, no such doubt is possible. Adapted from a book featuring a companion original to, and a Doctor substantially developed by, the Virgin range – a book which followed on directly from the events of its immediate predecessor, drew on elements of the series' mythology and continuity, and formed the fourth in Cornell's thematic 'English seasons' quartet – this television story is unequivocally influenced by the **New Adventures**. However much the story was altered in the process of adaptation (and it did change significantly, as we shall see), its narrative shape and style, its themes and politics, its ethos and aesthetic, were all crafted in the environment of mid-1990s literary **Doctor Who**.

On this occasion, **The Black Archive** has no choice but to pay attention to **Doctor Who** in book form. And this time, if you are at

[8] Gatiss wrote *The Unquiet Dead* (2005) and *The Idiot's Lantern* (2006); Jones wrote *The Impossible Planet / The Satan Pit* (2006); Roberts wrote *The Shakespeare Code* (2007) and *The Unicorn and the Wasp* (2008). Gatiss and Roberts continued to write scripts for Davies's successor, Steven Moffat.

all interested in the TV story *Human Nature / The Family of Blood*, you will need to as well.

CHAPTER 1: BOOK AND TELEVISION

Since *Human Nature / The Family of Blood* is in two parts rather than a single 45-minute episode, it is, like *Human Nature* [NA] itself, of considerable length. Many of the themes and content of the book are able to be preserved in the adaptation process, though transmuted into something new. Paul Cornell calls the TV story 'pretty much a straight adaptation' of the novel, in which 'the emotional journey's exactly the same'[9].

At first glance, the two versions of the story may appear very similar: at a small English boarding-school, shortly before the outbreak of the First World War, the Doctor becomes a human with no memory of his true identity; this alter ego, John Smith, falls in love but must regain his original self at the cost of this love, in order to protect the school, village, world and universe from a family of hostile aliens whose only loyalty is to themselves. However, a closer examination of the novel and TV story reveals that virtually no characters or incidents are precisely the same[10],

---

[9] Cornell, Paul, *Human Nature* [TV] DVD commentary.

[10] Of all the characters, only Rocastle and Hutchinson are little altered, though the latter's role in the story is very much diminished. The former loses his romantic interest in Joan, and the heroism of his death becomes more misguided (as he dies trying to save one of the Family, unaware that she is an alien duplicate, rather than in blowing one of them up). The incidents which come nearest to surviving intact run through the final First World War and Remembrance Day sequences, though as we shall see their emphasis has changed. (See Appendix 1 for further detail on character correspondences, and Appendix 4 for the more vexed question of whether the two versions of the story can be reconciled as both taking place in the same fictional universe.)

and it is the themes, outline and setting that are at the root of the adaptation. This first chapter will examine the story's origins as a novel, and the differences between its two versions; focussing on which changes are specifically tailored for the different media, which are due to the ongoing underlying narrative of **Doctor Who** and its progression between the two periods of publication and broadcast, and which reflect a more subtle adaptation of the narrative to explore new themes and ideas not necessarily present in the original. There may be overlap between these categories.

Transformative work

Some of the changes between the two versions are a consequence of the fact that they are fitted to the personalities of very different Doctors. Although explicitly the same character, the continuing plotlines of the seventh Doctor of *Human Nature* [NA] and the 10th Doctor of *Human Nature / The Family of Blood* put them in different circumstances. The results are very distinct, despite both being in character and rooted in the wider plotlines that surround the stories. This interacts with the fact that each iteration of the character is accompanied by a different companion, the implications of which are explored in more detail below.

Though simply an effect of the transition from one point in the series to another, and of the necessity to use the 'current' version of the Doctor, this imposed restriction on the story results in a very different expression of similar themes, in a way that is almost reminiscent of how transformative fan-produced work (such as fanfiction) can be used to explore alternate versions of existing characters or stories.

This similarity is not necessarily incidental. One could argue that the multi-authored and generational nature of **Doctor Who** means that almost any story written for it by someone who is a fan is a form of fanfiction, though there is a difference between officially sanctioned writing for a shared universe and fans writing for their own enjoyment. Cornell has stated that the concept for the novel originated in fanfiction he wrote when young, long before any thought of having it officially produced[11]. This is particularly interesting given that the structure of the story resonates with that of many transformative works created by fans for beloved media texts, both **Doctor Who** and others.

Cornell's own awareness of the book's position within a wider milieu which includes fanfiction is explicit in the fact that one of the chapters of *Human Nature* [NA] is titled 'Hurt/Comfort'. This phrase is the name for a common genre of fanfiction, wherein one of the characters is injured (or suffers psychologically) leading to them being cared for by another, often resulting in realisation of previously unspoken attraction or love. This is not coincidental; not only was Paul Cornell active in online fan communities and discussion, but he notes in his Acknowledgements that the story was developed in collaboration with Kate Orman, well known at the time as a writer of fanfiction for various series[12]. They would both have been well aware of these trends and terminologies.

---

[11] '[*Human Nature*] started life as fan fiction, before becoming a book in 1995 and finally, in 2007, a two-parter on television. "Something I wrote at school ended up on TV!" he said. "What am I going to do with the rest of my life?"' (Mills, Michael, '**Doctor Who** During the Wilderness Years').

[12] Cornell, Paul, *Human Nature* [NA] p271. 'Kate Orman', Fanlore.

It is not the hurt/comfort genre that is primarily exemplified in *Human Nature* [NA], but another very common method of transformation in the medium of fan works; the alternate universe story or 'AU'. These are stories in which the characters from a particular media work are transplanted to a different setting. There are many forms of this, from the diegetic way that characters might experience alternative universes in fantastical fiction (such as the alternative history Donna experiences in *Turn Left* (2008) or the 'Mirror universe' in **Star Trek**[13]) to a wholesale translation of the character to a different context. Archive of Our Own, one of the major sites for sharing of fanfiction, lists almost 30,000 works self-identified as 'High-school AU' (where the characters are re-imagined as schoolchildren) and over 68,000 listed as 'Alternate Universe – Modern setting'[14].

Lynn C, writing about the prevalence of AUs as a mode of storytelling in fan fiction, suggests that they are popular because they 'allow a greater variety of possible syntaxes than the source universe does.'[15] In other words, they broaden the scope of types of stories that can be told, while still allowing the core of the

[13] Introduced in the original series episode *Mirror, Mirror* (1967), and revisited during the course of **Star Trek: Deep Space Nine** (1993-99) and **Star Trek: Enterprise** (2001-05).

[14] Archive of our Own. These figures were collected in February 2017. It is important to note that these are specific categorisation terms in the tagging system. Other works with similar concepts may use slightly different terminology and therefore are not included in these figures.

[15] C, Lynn, 'Alternate Universes in Fan Fiction.' Presented at the annual conference of the International Association of the Fantastic in the Arts.

characters to be maintained; and character is often the critical aspect of fanfiction. These stories build on understanding established characters well enough to imagine how they would react plausibly in different circumstances. Although *Human Nature* is not strictly an AU in this sense, it does allow some of the same explorations to be made, because it enables us to understand more about the character of the Doctor by contrast with a different, constructed version of himself who nevertheless shares recognisable characteristics.

Cornell has several times mentioned that one of the major influences on his writing of *Human Nature* [NA] was a book from the **Star Trek: The Next Generation** tie-in range, *Imzadi* (1992) by Peter David[16]. Similar to the Virgin books for **Doctor Who**, these novels provided new stories for the familiar characters. *Imzadi* is generally regarded as one of the stand-out contributions to the range[17], and similarly used models of story construction familiar to readers and writers of fanfiction to explore new facets of the characters.

Part of this is, again, the use of alternate universes, this time more literally: a majority of the book takes place in the future of a

---

[16] For example: 'In many ways, it all started when I got onto the wrong train at Aylesbury station, and ended up waiting around at the wrong halt, with a copy of Peter David's **Star Trek: The Next Generation** novel, *Imzadi*' ('Introduction', *Human Nature* [NA], ebook, p341).

[17] For example: 'It's very easily the strongest **Next Generation** novel published while the show was on television, and remains a strong contender for the best **Next Generation** novel ever published.' Mooney, Darren, '**Star Trek: The Next Generation** – *Imzadi* by Peter David (Review)'.

different 'time stream' from the world portrayed in the television series. Will Riker reflects on the events that led to the death of Deanna Troi, which ultimately turns out to have never been meant to happen. This is an older, bitter version of the character, a 'what if' scenario that explores how critical Deanna is to his personal development. Unlike John Smith, this Admiral Riker is not a new blank slate created for the character, but a plausible endpoint for him given a particular set of tragic circumstances. But similarly, it provides insight into what makes the core of Will Riker, and what change is irrevocable. Indeed, on meeting him, the younger, 'real' Riker questions what could possibly have led him to such a place.

Imzadi shares another major similarity with fanfiction, in that it undertakes an exercise in 'filling in the blanks' in the characters' story. While Riker and Troi's introduction in *Encounter at Farpoint* (1987) mentions the fact that they have history together, it does not detail what this might be. Further episodes, for example *Haven* (1987), establish their romantic history, and the word 'Imzadi', first used in *Encounter at Farpoint* to describe their relationship, is translated as 'beloved'. *Imzadi* takes the history hinted at in the show, and transforms it into a fully-fleshed-out tale of young love, extrapolating from what was seen on screen[18]. Many transformative works, through building on strong interpersonal relations between characters, naturally bring romantic aspects into the stories. By using some of these strategies familiar from transformative works, *Human Nature* [NA] allows a move into a

[18] As can often happen with such fiction, this elaborated backstory would be contradicted by later episodes, such as *Second Chances* (1993).

genre that is not often seen in **Doctor Who**, or at least not with the eponymous lead at its heart: romance.

Who is the Doctor?

As described, many fan texts enjoy exploration of central characters having romantic relationships that are absent from, or only hinted at by, the original text. The term 'shipping', as coined by fans of **The X-Files** (1993-2002) in the 1990s, is now in common parlance[19] to describe this practice of imagining or re-examining relationships between characters. In the case of the Doctor, while we can presume that he has had relationships (from, for example, the fact that he has a granddaughter), this aspect of the character was seldom a prominent feature of his stories prior to the introduction of River Song in *Silence in the Library / Forest of the Dead* (2008). He seems, as a rule, to have little interest in romance or sexual encounters, which means that to explore this one must put him in a different context and mindset. Both *Human Nature* [NA] and *Human Nature / The Family of Blood* therefore allow this most human of experiences to be given to the Doctor without disrupting the normal context, an exploration via 'alternate self' of something that would normally be unavailable both to him and to the readers and viewers[20].

The two versions of the story express these departures from normality in different ways, however. For an example, we can look

---

[19] It is used, for instance, in *The Lego Batman Movie* (2017).

[20] Cornell acknowledges this fact in the commentary to *Human Nature* [TV] when he notes, in relation to Smith and Joan's first kiss, that 'there'll be fanfiction about this out there.' (*Human Nature* [TV] DVD commentary).

first at a detailed comparison between the openings of the novel and of the television story. The television episode starts in medias res, with the Doctor and Martha being chased with undeniable urgency and the high energy representative of the season. However the scene then cuts to an apparent awakening, and we see the 'normal' life of John Smith and his maid Martha. This sets up a question for the audience: where is the reality in what we are being presented with? Is the 'dream' real – as the cumulative context of the series will lead us to assume – or the incongruous 'awakening'? Immediately we are placed in a state of questioning which is not fully resolved until almost 20 minutes into the episode.

By contrast, the book opens in a very different place, with both the Doctor and his companion Bernice Summerfield ('Benny') in a state of melancholy and grief due to recent events:

> 'He had that troubled look about his eyes, and wouldn't quite look at me.
>
> 'I wanted rather desperately to touch him, hug him or something, but everything about him said that that wouldn't be a good idea. He seemed embarrassed about seeing me, which wasn't really him at all. If I didn't know better, I'd say that he was thinking as hard about the last five minutes of Guy's life as I was.'[21]

'Guy' is Guy de Carnac, a medieval Templar knight with whom Benny had a burgeoning romance in the previous novel in the range, *Sanctuary* by David A McIntee (1995). Guy is left fighting, protecting Benny and the Doctor, in a battle that almost certainly

---

[21] *Human Nature* [NA] p2.

results in his death. In the opening few pages of *Human Nature* [NA], the Doctor decides to travel to an alien market and make a purchase, which turns out to be the device that will transform him into John Smith: a character he has built out of the memories of previous companions.

In the book, therefore, the transformation to Smith is not presented as a mystery, nor as a result of conflict, but as a desirable state of change for the Doctor. We are not privy to his full reasons for making this change, but we can speculate that he is looking for a way of understanding the human condition to appreciate Benny and her recent tragedy more fully, and perhaps for an escape from his routine existence to a fantasised version of himself who lacks the problems that he is currently struggling with. Paul Cornell suggests the former interpretation: 'In the novel, it's left unclear why exactly he's done this to himself, though there's a dirty great hint that it's to share and understand Benny's emotional state.'[22]

We will explore the idea of escape more closely later on.

The divergent openings not only place each story within the context of the ongoing narrative, but set up an appropriate catalyst for the story that unfolds. The seventh Doctor, who in the Virgin novels in particular is represented as a masterful strategist, is the agent of his own transformation. He appears to be looking for a means to create change, and the opening is an exploration of this state of mind. The 10th Doctor on the other hand is pushed into this scenario; though not fully without enthusiasm. 'Never thought

---

[22] Cornell, Paul, 'Adapting the Novel for the Screen', *Human Nature* [NA], ebook, p360.

I'd use this... all the times I've wondered,' he says, indicating that this is perhaps an excuse for something he has, for some reason, otherwise denied himself. Even the pain associated with it, something Martha queries, is presented almost gleefully: 'Oh yeah... it hurts.'[23]

(It is also interesting, given the urgency with which the Chameleon Arch transformation seems to be approached, to consider when the Doctor might have made the recording which he leaves for Martha with instructions on how to proceed. Was this made previously, with the implication that he always intended to use the Arch to become human at some point? This seems somewhat unlikely, given he refers specifically to their flight from those seeking them. Does it happen at some ambiguous moment in the pursuit, or before the change from the Arch fully takes hold? Or perhaps even at a future point, which brings up the question of why those specific instructions were issued?)

These differences highlight how the same story can be told effectively with significantly different characterisation for the protagonist. The lack of melancholia is not simply a consequence of the lighter tone required for a family-suitable television broadcast, thought that is undoubtedly a factor. Unlike that of the manipulative seventh Doctor, the state of the 10th Doctor could be understood as one of denial rather than contemplation. The actions shown in each version of the story, as well as putting a different emphasis on the reasons for the change, are representative of the different character aspects in these two incarnations. As we will explore in more depth in the next chapter, the 10th Doctor's

---

[23] *Human Nature* [TV].

impulse to flee could be read as a reaction to his comparatively recent experiences in the Time War (and his loss of Rose), and as representing a means of repression rather than acknowledgement. Two different stories are being told here from a similar conceptual starting-point, and while both reflect on the necessity of conflict and war, it can be suggested that they come to quite different conclusions in terms of message and moral imperative.

Equally, when the Doctor returns to his true self at the end of the story, we see differences in how the respective characterisations affect his actions and behaviour. There are three key events which take place at the end of both versions: the Doctor's conversation with Joan about the distinctions between himself and John Smith; his defeat of the villainous family; and the coda with the elderly Tim. While the divergences in how these unfold are significant in regard to how they reflect the character of the Doctor, they are also highly tied to the differing roles of these supporting characters, as will be explored when we look below at how these are portrayed.

The Role of the Companion

Another major difference in the direction that the adaptation takes is the companion's role in the story. This is in part necessitated by how the historical context interacts with the different attributes of Benny and Martha. Benny's cover identity was as the niece of John Smith, but this is not a role that Martha could plausibly have filled. Her and the 10th Doctor's apparent ages would have argued against it (although a niece eight years younger than her uncle would have been far from unknown in the Victorian era, when she and Smith would notionally have been born), but more significantly she and the Doctor are of different ostensible ethnicities[24]. This necessitates a change that brings the story in new directions, and allows different aspects of the historical setting to be the focus of the companion's storyline.

Both companions are required to act to protect the interests of the Doctor in his 'absence', and are given authority to act on his behalf. In both versions, instructions are left hurriedly to guide the way, although we see these more completely in the novel, and they are used to very different purposes in terms of how the two companions deal with the unfolding relationship between Smith and Joan Redfern. While Martha bemoans the fact the list does not include the contingency, Benny adds 'Don't let me fall in love' to the end of it[25].

The internal conflict in Benny's primary plotline arises from her greater remove from the time period and her lack of ability (or will) to hide this from contemporary people she is meeting and living among. The interactions that Benny has with various characters serve to highlight her lack of familiarity with the historical period and its mores due to her wider chronological distance from it. Since Benny is from the 26th century, she makes errors understanding slang and context, some more serious than others.

---

[24] Freema Agyeman is of Ghanaian and Iranian parentage, and in theory it would seem feasible for Martha to be the daughter of Smith's brother or sister with a black spouse. In 1913 this would have been implausible socially, rather than genetically. (Compare with Bill's claim in *Knock Knock* – broadcast and set in 2017 – that the Doctor is her grandfather, which is accepted by her friends as perfectly reasonable.)

[25] *Human Nature* [TV]; *Human Nature* [NA] p175.

While the Doctor is happily oblivious in his role as John Smith, she struggles both with operating effectively in early 20th-century society, and with the guilt of revealing (or concealing) what is to her historical knowledge, but is yet to come for the friends she makes.

The challenges of existing in this time period are evidenced in particular by the looming First World War, and by the social upheaval of the women's suffrage movement. This intersects at several points with Benny's plotlines – particularly in the person of Constance, a character who does not appear in the television adaptation, but whose place (as a confidante later impersonated by one of the aliens) is in part taken by Jenny. Constance is an active campaigner who has been jailed and (helpfully for the plot) has access to explosives. When Benny changes into anachronistic clothing, she is mistaken as being part of the same suffrage movement. Yet while this behaviour gains Benny attention, it does not provoke the same kind of discrimination as Martha experiences, and in fact is a choice made by Benny to present herself with anachronistic behaviours.

Martha, by contrast, is given in her storyline only tangential commentary on suffrage (she has a conversation with Jenny about the voting rights of women, and the fact that they are not allowed inside the pub) but is better placed to highlight the intersectional aspects of class, race and gender which affect her as a working-class black woman in pre-War England. Her role as a maid makes sense as a context in which she would be able to associate closely with Smith, but it also provides conflict, and exposes her to the systemic and individual racism of the period. This is implicit very early on in *Human Nature* [TV]:

MARTHA

Not everyone's that considerate, what with me being...

GESTURES AT HER FACE

JENNY

A Londoner?

Martha's societal role in relation to Smith and other characters is explored further as we move through the episode, in particular when she is required to take on a leadership position in resistance against the Family. Her actions are rejected by Smith as she is just 'a servant', and he behaves in a racist and patronising fashion when imagining she does not understand the difference between fact and fiction[26]. When, later, she talks of her true identity as a medical professional, the importance of race as well as gender is highlighted by Joan's response: 'Women might train to be doctors, but hardly a skivvy, and hardly one of your colour.'[27]

Unlike the confused but fond relationship Smith has with Benny, Martha's 'familiarity' with him is unacceptable and socially anachronous. This one-sided relationship between Martha and Smith echoes 2007's ongoing storyline of Martha's unreciprocated and mostly unspoken feelings for the Doctor, which she acknowledges when she catches him in a kiss with Joan and is visibly upset: 'You had to go and fall in love with a human... and it wasn't me.'[28] Smith cares for Martha, but only as servant who is part of his daily life and has limited agency and authority. Similarly,

---

[26] *Human Nature* [TV].
[27] *The Family of Blood*.
[28] *Human Nature* [TV].

one could take this as a reflection of how Martha perceives her relationship to the Doctor. He is alien and unattainable, but not unquestionably so; she is aware that Rose occupies a privileged place in his history, and had an extremely close relationship with him (note how she is mentioned in Smith's 'Journal of Impossible Things' at the start of the story). Rose represents an avenue of hope that perhaps this distance is an illusion and the Doctor may one day notice Martha in the same way.

The nature of love is therefore a key theme for both the Doctor and companion in both versions of the story; but while Martha's story is focussed on the nature of unrequited love and the inability to choose who one has feelings for, Benny's can be read as more about whether love is worth the pain that comes when it is lost. This can be seen through the subplot surrounding Alexander Shuttleworth, a character who has no correlate in the television version. Alexander accidently learns, through use of technology Benny brings with her, of the forthcoming death in war of his beloved, Richard Hadleman. Although it is not stated outright, and Benny does not understand the nature of the context for most of the book because of her misreading of historical cues, Alexander's love for Richard, and his foreknowledge of his death, provide a comparison to Benny's experience of Guy's unconfirmed death – neither of the two are precisely dead at this moment, but from a different perspective both died long ago. Therefore we can suggest that, while the television version of the story is about love not realised or fulfilled, the book is about the death of love.

Another result of this shift of role for Martha is the position it puts her in with respect to Joan, creating more of a rivalry than exists in the book version.

Smith and Joan

The character of Joan is critical to both versions of the story, and she seems at first glance to be one of the few consistent characters, as the pacifistic, apparently innocent, widow who falls in requited love with John Smith[29]. But in fact there are key differences between the two versions, which again impact on the wider themes of the stories.

In the book, Joan is a science teacher; an educational role which puts her in a position of knowledge and authority, and makes her an intellectual equal with Smith. In the television version, she is the school matron. This sets her slightly apart from the teachers at the school, in a position that is highly coded as feminine in this time period, and presents her as a nurturing figure both for the boys in the school and John. This makes for a different dynamic between her and the Doctor, emphasising his (from the audience's point of view) outdatedly patriarchal attitudes which are demonstrated elsewhere in the episode, and also facilitating a specific conflict between her and Martha, who uses her knowledge as a 21st-

---

[29] Interestingly, the need for Smith to give Joan up recalls the original series **Star Trek** episode *The City on the Edge of Forever* (1967), which provides the mechanism used for time-travel in David's *Imzadi*, and which that book references extensively (for instance on pp3-4, 8, 261 and 342). In the episode, Captain Kirk visits 1930s New York where he falls in love with a woman, Edith Keeler, played by Joan Collins. Unfortunately – and in contrast with Deanna's unscheduled death in *Imzadi* – history requires Edith to die young, and Kirk must allow this if he is to preserve the future in which the United Federation of Planets exists. Notably, Edith is a pacifist – her influence would have kept the USA from entering the Second World War – and is played by a woman named Joan.

century medical student to display an anachronistic level of education and proficiency. This begins early in the first episode when Martha asks if Smith has a concussion and Joan suggest she 'knows more about it', before we even know the specifics of the situation[30].

Ironically however, it is the television version of Joan who is more assertive and takes a leadership role: who brings Smith and Martha to the empty Cartwright house, who convinces Smith he really may be the Doctor, and who takes the initiative in the dance hall and leads the people to safety, after Smith is seemingly frozen in fear despite Martha's urgent instructions. As Martha tells him, 'God, you're rubbish as a human.'

While Joan does seem to accept that Martha has the knowledge she claims, she does not let it diminish her own importance: 'I might not be a doctor but I'm still their nurse. They need me.'[31] Joan appears to be stronger than Smith is, despite the assumptions that might be made about her and her role.

As mentioned above, Joan's relationship with Martha is different from the one her novel equivalent has with Benny. Benny has no romantic aspirations towards the Doctor, and is presented as Smith's niece. Having checked that it is not one of the things he forbade himself in the instructions he gave her, she does not object to his seeking a love-affair, though she thinks that it is 'odd' and later seems to feel sad about the fact that it is by nature going to be short and ultimately unrequited[32]. Eventually, as mentioned

---

[30] *Human Nature* [TV].
[31] *The Family of Blood.*
[32] *Human Nature* [NA] pp47, 180.

above, Benny adds a handwritten note to the end of the list to try to convince him it was not something he would want, to little effect. Despite her impartiality, she is not as sympathetic to Joan as one might expect given the circumstances: instead they clash in terms of worldview. Benny refers to Joan as a 'wrinkly racist'[33] and does not appear to understand the appeal that she holds for Smith. (Towards the end of the book, she does seem more accepting of the idea and even offers to be a bridesmaid if the wedding were to take place[34].) Martha on the other hand tells Joan she is just the Doctor's friend and not her rival, though she cuts off before finishing the thought that she wishes she was[35].

Benny's evidence for the literary Joan's racism is presumably the Irish joke she has just made[36]. In the original 1995 edition, Joan earlier referred (though not in Benny's hearing) to 'A nigger band'[37], but one of the reissue's few textual amendments excises the racial epithet in favour of 'Some harmony group'[38]. Oddly, Smith's instinctive cringe in response to the word (evidently inherited from the Doctor) remains in the revised text, though now lacking any discernible cause. In any case, the novel Joan's racism is apparently limited to careless words – she shows no obvious prejudice, for instance, towards Timothy's Indian classmate Anand.

---

[33] *Human Nature* [NA] p180.
[34] *Human Nature* [NA] p232.
[35] *The Family of Blood*.
[36] *Human Nature* [NA] p179.
[37] *Human Nature* [NA], 1995 ed, p128.
[38] *Human Nature* [NA], 2015 ed, p136. The ebook has the transitional 'A n– band', together with a lengthy note from Cornell on why he originally used the word, and why the change was made (*Human Nature* [NA], ebook, pp173, 350-51).

The television Joan's racism in response to Martha seems more self-aware and personal.

It is interesting to note, though, that both Martha and Benny appear to feel a degree of pity for Joan, as well as disdain. The companion in each storyline has the privileged information, as does the audience, that this relationship will not outlast the adventure: the character of the Doctor does not appear to allow for love and marriage in the way that Joan would expect, and demand[39]. This, then, is the central conflict of this relationship: it is an illusion that can never be made reality in the long term.

The difference between the two relationships, in the original and the adaptation, is most explicit in the confrontation that takes place at the end of each story. At the end of *Human Nature* [NA], Benny forces the restored Doctor to go and talk to Joan, something he is reluctant to do; it is suggested that without her prompting he would have left without speaking to her, and is uncomfortable with further interaction. We do not see a similar scene in *The Family of Blood* and it seems that the Doctor has made this decision on his own.

Joan in the book pleads with the man who resembles her beloved, and tries to convince him that he must be capable of love:

> '"But you don't love me?"
>
> '"No. I can't."
>
> '"Why? Is he not a part of you? The human part?"

---

[39] Even his later married life with River Song is hardly conventional in early 20th-century terms.

'"There is no human part. I'm a Time Lord. A different species. He was a character I created, a fiction."'[40]

The Doctor claims that person she loved never really existed, but also acknowledges that Smith is an individual, separate from himself, who 'died', nobly, and could not be restored; even if he were to repeat the process of becoming a human, he tells her, he would not be John.

The televisual Joan, on the other hand, accepts immediately that the Doctor is not John Smith, despite the Doctor telling her that Smith is a part of himself, that 'everything that John Smith is and was, I'm capable of that too'. For the 10th Doctor, his own survival at the expense of John's is a conscious choice that he makes, in the absence of threat.

JOAN

Where is he? John Smith?

DOCTOR

He's in here somewhere.

JOAN

Like a story. Could you change back?

DOCTOR

Yes.

JOAN

Will you?

---

[40] *Human Nature* [NA] p256.

DOCTOR

No.

Despite that, he tries to retain those aspects of the relationship that he can understand. In a display of insensitivity, he asks her to travel with him as his companion, and says he wants to 'try, at least.' But she refuses: 'John Smith is dead, and you look like him'. She also points out to him his culpability in the deaths that have occurred, since he came to them and brought peril 'on a whim'. It is clear that Joan does not think the Doctor is worth her love, or even her respect, and that to her he is not and never will be John[41].

It is hard to say which is the more tragic figure: the Doctor who claims to be incapable of love but regrets his loss of it, or the one who claims that he could recreate it but fails to understand why that is impossible.

The Family of Blood

Themes of family run very strongly through both versions of the story[42], and are foregrounded particularly in the nature of the villains. There are significant differences in how they are portrayed in each version: the Aubertides of the novel, although superficially similar to the Family of Blood, are very different in detail.

Firstly, their relationship to the process of the 'humanisation' of a Time Lord entails a very different agency in the story. In the novel, the Aubertides have prepared a trap for any Time Lord that they happen to come across, offering a new physiology, personality and set of memories to an unwary Gallifreyan. They appear to be

[41] *The Family of Blood*.
[42] See Chapter 3 for more on this.

flexible in terms of how this is used, noting that, counter to their expectations, the Doctor has provided the character and details of John Smith himself (as opposed, in the adaptation, to the character being built by the TARDIS), having constructed it from the memories and experiences of his companions. Their motivation is to enable them to possess the capabilities of a Time Lord in order to increase their reproductive capacity, with additional regeneration cycles allowing them to break out of their innate limit of six offspring.

By contrast, we do not learn specific details about the motivation of the Family of Blood, other than that they are hunting the Doctor and Martha, can 'smell' a Time Lord across time and space, and are seeking for themselves immortality.

The television version of the Family initially appear as an incorporeal mist, and do not have any firm appearance of their own: as they say, 'We go through shapes so very fast.'[43] However, rather than having bodies that can be adapted to different appearances, as is the case with the Aubertides, the Family solely take over existing humans. Here, the little girl with a balloon is a simulacrum of the Cartwright girl, and the balloon just a balloon, rather than the terrible weapon described in the book. Although both versions are horrifying in their behaviours, the television Family are less subtle, somewhat cartoonish villains with unclear motivations. By contrast, while sociopathic in their disregard for others, the book's Aubertides have immense loyalty and love for their own family and display this frequently. They are said to be anomalous for their species, which is generally peaceable.

[43] *Human Nature* [TV].

Interestingly then, given the greater scope for pity which might seem to be provided by the misguided Aubertides, it is the Family who get arguably more sympathetic treatment at the end of the television story, as 'Baines' narrates his horror at the punishments the Doctor, in his anger, metes out: 'He never raised his voice; that was the worst thing [...] We wanted to live forever, so the Doctor made sure that we did.'[44]

Those Aubertides who survive the original version of the story are not punished, nor treated with mercy, but rather disposed of almost as a nuisance. Two of them are imprisoned within the cricket-ball-shaped 'Biodatapod' that formerly contained the Doctor's consciousness, and are sent to be securely guarded[45]. A third escapes punishment, having, it is implied, betrayed the family to the Time Lords[46]. A fourth is given over to the custody of the human authorities, with a warning not to let him eat meat, as he can take the form of any organism whose DNA he ingests[47]:

> '"Don't be barbarous. Oh, he might get away –" the Doctor tapped his umbrella handle against his chin – "but what will he do? He's got no weapons, no technology, and a life span of, what, ten more years at most? That's the thing about such powerful biosystems. They burn themselves out." His face darkened. "I think killing him would be far too merciful."'[48]

---

[44] *The Family of Blood.*
[45] *Human Nature* [NA] pp248, 251.
[46] *Human Nature* [NA] pp258-59.
[47] *Human Nature* [NA] pp128, 253.
[48] *Human Nature* [NA] pp252-53. It is implied that Greeneye gets his comeuppance nevertheless: in custody he requests 'a corned-

The specific reasons for this difference, and the motivation for the Doctor's vengeance (which some may say would seem out of character) will be explored in Chapter 4.

Timothy: Psychic, or Young Time Lord?

Both the book and the television episodes have a version of the character Tim (surnamed Latimer on TV and Dean in the book[49]), who provides a viewpoint character to follow the hidden world of schoolboys as a contrast to the role of John Smith the teacher. In the book, there is an extended storyline relating to Tim's experience of being severely bullied – the extent and nature of which mean that it was likely considered unsuitable for the family nature of a television version.

But Tim's connection to the story is also different in part because of the mechanism of transformation; in the book, he is drawn to the Doctor's Time Lord essence as contained in the Pod, and begins to take on aspects of a Time Lord, both physiological and psychical. These include the mystical connections which are an ongoing element of Paul Cornell's **New Adventures** and of the series as a whole, picked up on by several authors. By contrast, in the television version, we have the Chameleon Arch, something that also serves to foreshadow longer-reaching storylines that span the 2007 season[50]. Though Timothy does appear drawn to the pocket watch and steals it (and perhaps, by opening it, draws the attention

---

beef sandwich', and 80 years later Timothy's great-granddaughter recounts an urban legend of a cow once found in a prison cell and sent to the abattoir (*Human Nature* [NA] pp259, 268).

[49] *Human Nature* [TV], *Human Nature* [NA] p24.

[50] See in particular *Utopia* (2007).

of the Family) it appears almost as if he is protecting the watch, and by extension the Doctor. It asks him to keep it safe, and keep it closed because 'The time is not right.'[51] Again, medium (and audience) make a difference but this also changes the character of John Smith's actions towards Tim. In both, it is Smith's place to argue for the necessity of war and the need not to be perceived as 'other', against Tim's pacifism and nonconformity, contrasting with the position the Doctor would normally take in these debates. It is also important to note that the TV Tim's latent psychic abilities are extant even before he comes into contact with the Doctor: 'Sometimes I say things and they turn out to be correct.'[52]

This ability to glimpse the future gives an opportunity to explore characters' impressions of the oncoming War. In the book these were enabled by the 'time barrier' which is erected around the town and causes similar effects (a storyline mostly abandoned elsewhere in the adaptation). In both versions, it is implied that a change is made to the future timeline by the actions of Timothy. But whereas on television direct action by Tim as a result of his glimpses of the future leads him to save Hutchinson, in the book Hutchinson dies in the manner that Tim predicted, and it is Richard Hadleman who is saved – by the presence of Tim as a member of the Red Cross, not as a soldier. This rejection of warfare in favour of healing carries through into the book's present-day coda, in which the elderly Tim is wearing a white poppy. In the television version, however, the more familiar (and ambiguously coded) red poppy is worn. The specific messages regarding war and conflict will form the focus of the next chapter.

---

[51] *The Family of Blood*.
[52] *Human Nature* [TV].

So far, we have been looking at the differences in how the same base story is treated across the two media. However, despite the many changes required by the transition, the broad strokes of the story do remain the same and one might argue that the underlying messages are, if not identical, then transmuted in interesting ways from the same base material. In the following chapters we will pick out the major themes which are apparent in *Human Nature / The Family of Blood* and examine how the treatment of them differs, and whether this affects the underlying concepts being conveyed.

CHAPTER 2: WAR AND PEACE

As we have seen in Chapter 1, war is a major, explicit theme in both versions of the story. However, the approach to this theme has seen significant changes in the adaptation process, and what appears on screen must be considered on its own terms. In this chapter we will examine how the television adaptation approaches depictions of conflict, while contrasting it with the original version when the two diverge significantly. We will look at how this relates to the interpretation of the Doctor's character, and how it fits into wider themes of conflict in the series as a whole.

Doctor Who has frequently touched on themes of war throughout its run; this would seem almost inevitable in a series which covers large spans of history and geography and, as an adventure-drama, often places the protagonists in situations of conflict. Examples of this are many and various, from the religious conflicts of *The Crusade* (1965) to the pyrotechnic space battles of *The Time of the Doctor* (2013), but particularly in the context of *Human Nature / The Family of Blood*'s placement in the wider narrative of **Doctor Who**, we need to emphasise the importance of the Time War.

The backstory to the 2005 revival of the series was a war in which the Doctor was not a neutral observer swept up in events, working towards a reconciliation between the parties, or even conscripted to support one side or the other, but a combatant with a personal stake, and with a major role in ending the hostilities through violent action. Many depictions of the Doctor seem to position him as a pacifist[53], so the revelation of him as an (albeit unwilling)

---

[53] For a recent example, see Chapter 3 of Purser-Hallard, Philip, *The Black Archive #4: Dark Water / Death in Heaven* (2016).

warrior and soldier is an interesting choice. It is one that informed Russell T Davies' revival from the start, and continues to contribute throughout the series, culminating in the revelations in *The Day of the Doctor* (2013) that his role was not the one that he, or others, thought. There are many points in the 21st-century run where this juxtaposition is questioned, for example positioning Peter Capaldi's 12th Doctor as explicitly antagonistic to soldiers in the aftermath of the revelation of the existence and repression of the War Doctor. But in the chronology of *Human Nature / The Family of Blood*, we are in a position where the Doctor still grapples with the ultimate survivor's guilt; not only that he alone survived the genocide of his species, but that he was responsible for it.

While this character history is not always referenced explicitly in individual episodes, instead dropping into the background for large stretches, it inevitably influences how writers interpret the character. The Time War and its consequences become foregrounded at the end of the 2007 season, with the revelation of the Master's survival of the War, and how he and the Doctor were impacted by it[54]. A handful of episodes prior to this, *Human Nature / The Family of Blood* serves a key foreshadowing purpose by introducing the idea of the Chameleon Arch and pocket watch, by which method the Master also hides himself. Given that Cornell acknowledges that the watch as an alternative to the Pod was an idea which came from Davies[55], it seems reasonable to speculate that placing this in the context of an episode that also examines the Doctor's character in relation to war and conflict is not incidental.

---

[54] In *Utopia, The Sound of Drums* and *Last of the Time Lords* (all 2007).

[55] Cornell, 'Adapting the Novel for the Screen', p361.

Attitudes to Warfare

Presentation of war is complex in media, in part because the topic itself is a complex one. While very few would ever argue that war is a 'good' thing, militarism may be painted as something necessary and worthwhile. This is particularly the case with the two World Wars: the First World War in particular is known as the 'Great War', which is in part a reference to its unprecedented scale, but also reflects the frequent portrayal of those who fought in it, and their cause, as righteous and heroic – even if other aspects were not. Part of this may be a sense of nostalgia; as combatants fall out of living memory they are held up as heroes of the past rather than contemporaries who must be held responsible for consequences. Similarly, in depictions of the Second World War, focus is often on the heroism and fortitude of combatants[56]. This is in contrast to the depiction of other, more recent wars such as those involving the USA in Korea and Vietnam, which are far more likely to be portrayed critically and shown as unjust, unnecessary, evil and cruel. It is the veterans of these modern, ambiguous wars who are more likely to be portrayed as 'going off the rails'[57].

Human Nature / The Family of Blood appears at first glance to be critical of war, which would seem consistent with the commonly perceived characterisation of the Doctor as a pacifist, who rejects military involvement and use of weapons. Historically the Doctor's relationship with guns has been a complex one, ranging from

---

[56] For example **Band of Brothers** (2001), which, while depicting the horrors of war, does so through the lens of individual soldiers' experiences and relationships.

[57] Certainly in American media, where this is a recurrent television plotline.

casually firing one to kill (the third Doctor in *Day of the Daleks* (1972)), through using one as leverage by threatening **himself** (the eighth Doctor in *Doctor Who* (1996)) to repudiating their use altogether (the fourth Doctor in *Pyramids of Mars* (1975) and *The Robots of Death* (1977)[58]). Despite such befuddling inconsistency, the declarative nature of the Doctor's anti-gun speeches has led to this disavowal being seen as a touchstone of the character, to the extent that the *TV Tropes* website introduces its 'Doesn't Like Guns' page with this fairly typical exchange from *Army of Ghosts* (2006):

ROSE

> Doctor, they've got guns.

DOCTOR

> And I haven't. Which makes me the better person, don't you think? They can shoot me dead, but the moral high ground is mine.

Generally, however, Russell T Davies' two Doctors fall at the rejectionist end of the spectrum; though they may be happy to handle guns briefly, generally to relieve an opponent of them[59], and may even use them to threaten an enemy before disavowing any intention of ever using them[60], they contemplate firing a gun only under conditions of extreme mental distress, such as when the

---

[58] He tells Sarah 'I never carry firearms' in the former and Leela 'I never carry weapons' in the latter (episode 1 in both cases), although both women see him do so shortly afterwards (in *The Seeds of Doom* (1976) and *The Talons of Weng-Chiang* (1977)).
[59] For instance in *The Sontaran Stratagem* (2008).
[60] For instance in *Bad Wolf* (2005) and *The Doctor's Daughter* (2008).

ninth Doctor learns that the Daleks are no longer extinct, or when the 10th makes a similar discovery about the Time Lords[61].

There are several points during *Human Nature / The Family of Blood* where sympathetic characters are critical of militarism and conflict, in contrast to the presumed historical context as represented by the setting and other characters. As a stand-in character for the Doctor[62], Tim's is one of these sympathetic viewpoints. The scene at the shooting range is the first to show us to any major extent the difference between how Tim feels about war, and how the other characters are prone to the glorification of it – even John Smith. Tim is not directly firing the gun, but is asked to provide support by feeding in the bullets. But still he baulks, because he feels the injustice of the disparity between his side and the supposed enemy, even if at this point they are simply pretending. While this is not interrogated as heavily in the television version as it is in the book, the implication is that Tim is more aligned in his attitudes to those of the Doctor and thus those the audience should aspire to – but this provides a shocking contrast to John Smith, who does not appear to see any issues with the situation as presented. In fact rather than supporting Tim, he gives his approval for punishment over his behaviour.

The firing-range scene, and Tim's ambivalence towards the weapon, prefigure Smith's behaviour in the battle scene in *The Family of Blood*. Here John Smith is clearly handling his gun with the intention of using it against the scarecrows and the Family; equally clearly, he chooses not to. Whether this is because the

---

[61] *Dalek*, *The End of Time* Part 2 (2010).
[62] See Chapter 1.

battle scene being played out in front of him reignites the trauma of the Time War (unremembered by Smith but possibly inherited from the Doctor), or due to belated stirrings of pacifist morality, we cannot tell. Nevertheless, the image of Tennant's character holding a gun – as much as that of him training boys to use one in the prior episode – is a marker of how far John Smith has deviated from the norms established for the Doctor during Davies' time as showrunner.

The only person at the firing range who seems to share Tim's disgust at the scenario of schoolboys being taught to kill is Joan, who is reminded distastefully of the war that took her husband from her. In the episodes, Joan represents another alternative viewpoint, questioning the need for violence and conflict. In the conversation following the occurrences on the shooting range, she expresses her anger with the army for depriving her of her husband (with Smith noting that the anger is still present and not simply something from the past), and questions the necessity of the exercise and even its usefulness.

SMITH

> Don't you think discipline is good for them?

JOAN

> Does it have to be such military discipline? I mean, if there's another war those boys won't find it so amusing.

Her admonishment elicits a more moderate response from Smith, which he expresses just before exhibiting some very Doctor-like behaviour:

SMITH

> And I'll admit mankind doesn't need warfare and bloodshed to prove itself. Everyday life can provide honour and valour, and let's hope that from now on this… this country can find its heroes in smaller places.

In the sequence that follows, where he saves a child with the throw of a cricket ball, he seems energised by his behaviour, and inspired to ask Joan to the dance[63]. One could suggest that his reversion to 'himself' gives him confidence, but then again making a romantic overture is not necessarily something that the Doctor would do.

Joan's standpoint with regard to warfare also becomes significant at the conclusion of the story, where she is called upon to help Smith make a choice: whether to remain as himself or return to being the Doctor in the name of stopping the Family. Smith's journal gives Joan insight into the possible future in which the Family are not stopped, and acquire the fob watch:

SMITH

> If they get what they want, then, then…

JOAN

> Then it all ends in destruction. I never read to the end, but those creatures would live forever to breed and conquer. A war across the stars for every child.[64]

It is Joan who convinces Smith that he needs to take action for the greater good and to prevent war – but it is sacrifice (for them both)

---

[63] *Human Nature* [TV].
[64] *The Family of Blood*.

rather than combat that is required of him. The flash of awareness of their possible life together highlights what they are giving up. While she believes that the Doctor will not love her, she also believes that the man she loves, John Smith, will do what is right.

From this we might conclude that both Tim and Joan are positioned to deliver anti-war arguments within the narrative. However, in contrast perhaps to the novel, this message is not so clear by the end of the episode, as we shall see below. The question of whether fighting is sometimes necessary is examined more deeply in both the book and television versions, with potentially differing conclusions.

Foregrounding War

In order to emphasise the themes that are central to the story, the episodes *Human Nature* [TV] and *The Family of Blood* contain many explicit mentions of war, both historical wars in the context of the 1913 setting, and future wars both actual and potential. The majority of the story takes place on 11 November[65], which from 1918 will become Armistice Day, though the period characters are of course unaware of this. The first scene with John Smith fulfilling his role as a teacher shows him taking a history class, teaching about the Napoleonic Wars and the Battle of Waterloo. This immediately sets up John Smith as someone who is familiar with how wars have started, and their consequences. Presenting him as

---

[65] In the pre-credits sequence Martha tells Smith, 'It's Monday November 10th 1913'. The sighting of the Family's spaceship apparently takes place that night, meaning that the rest of *Human Nature* [TV] takes place during Tuesday 11 November, and most of *The Family of Blood* during the night that follows.

having this detailed knowledge of military history could conceivably have given him greater insight into why and how war should be avoided, but his attitudes later in the episode do not seem to support this. Martha, on the other hand, is very aware of the historical context of where she is, and what is coming. In her first scene, she considers the future, or lack of it, that potentially awaits the boys who are taunting her:

JENNY

> Just think, though. In a few years' time, boys like that'll be running the country.

MARTHA

> 1913. They might not.

John Smith also talks to Tim directly about warfare, recommending to him a book on the Siege of Mafeking (1899-1900) that includes 'fascinating details'[66]. It's worth noting that the siege (which was still recent in 1913) involved 12 to 15-year-old boys of the 'Mafeking Cadet Corps' acting as orderlies, and the use of various tactics to deceive the besieging forces into believing more troops held the town than were actually there; and that while the relief of the besieged town was lauded in Britain as a significant victory, in terms of the larger Boer War effort it was ineffective and considered a waste of resources. There is therefore a dual purpose in this reference: introducing the idea that Smith is trying to encourage his pupils to consider tactics and strategy (which will become relevant to the events later in the episode) and using a particular example where there was no clear victor.

---

[66] *Human Nature* [TV].

These and other small reminders of war as a key context reoccur throughout the pair of episodes, for example in the presence of the veteran of the Crimean War (1853-56) taking a collection outside the dance hall; although distant from the period in question, his presence illustrates that the conflict remains in living memory[67].

But we also get several explicit mentions of the Great War that will plague the world in the short-term future. The Family are aware of future history, which they have looked at and seem to call judgement upon:

'BAINES'

All your little tin soldiers. But tell me, sir, will they thank you?

ROCASTLE

I don't understand.

'BAINES'

What do you know of history, sir? What do you know of next year?

ROCASTLE

You're not making sense, Baines.

'BAINES'

1914, sir. Because the Family has travelled far and wide looking for Mr Smith and, oh, the things we have seen. War is coming. In foreign fields, war of the whole wide world,

[67] Though the veteran would clearly have to be in his 70s at least.

with all your boys falling down in the mud. Do you think they will thank the man who taught them it was glorious?[68]

Even before this, though, the probable fate of the boys in the school is highlighted in the scenes where they are trained in the use of weapons which they will most likely be asked to use during the War. Joan, who has read Smith's 'Journal of Impossible Things', reflects on how this might impact their futures:

JOAN

In your journal, in one of your stories, you wrote about next year. 1914.

SMITH

That was just a dream.

JOAN

All those images of mud and wire. You told of a shadow. A shadow falling across the entire world.

SMITH

Well then, they can be thankful it's not true.

This constant reference to the real, historical wars which surround the setting of the episode ground it with a realism not often seen in **Doctor Who**, which allows the episode to address broader themes of war in a way that, unlike elsewhere in the series, is neither allegorical (through the more explicit involvement of the characters in a fictional war) nor oblique in its reference to real history.

---

[68] *The Family of Blood*.

What Makes a Coward?

In the previous chapter, we noted that the character of Tim, and his journey, are quite different between the two versions; however his story purpose remains. He acts as an advocate of non-violent conflict resolution, and an avatar of the Doctor (both figuratively and to some extent literally) in a story in which the latter is absent.

In the scene where he lends Tim the book on Mafeking, Smith also tells him that 'no man should hide himself,' which is not only an unknowing allusion to his own hidden condition, but reflects on Tim's choices later[69]. Tim is scolded or mocked by others throughout the episodes for being cowardly, which serves to highlight an alternative view of conflict – that it is not to be glorified and sought out, but rather something that might be avoided by using alternative tactics.

HUTCHINSON

Latimer, you filthy coward!

TIM

Oh yes, sir. Every time.[70]

The distinction between cowardice on the one hand, and retreat or active refusal to engage on the other, is an interesting one. It is worth noting as a reflection of how **Doctor Who** has approached conflict and warfare, but also more broadly in terms of the Doctor as a character. The descriptor 'never cruel or cowardly' is one that has often been attached to the Doctor (and is alluded to several

---

[69] *Human Nature* [TV].
[70] *The Family of Blood*.

times in *Human Nature* [NA][71]), but is not necessarily always a credo to which he adheres. One of the most noticeable things about the end of this story is that the punishments meted out to the Family could in fact be considered cruel, going beyond justice and into retribution, as we will discuss further in Chapter 4. In *Bad Wolf / The Parting of the Ways* (2005), the ninth Doctor expresses a sentiment very similar to Tim's, when presented with a choice echoing that which he made in the Time War:

EMPEROR DALEK

I want to see you become like me. Hail the Doctor, the Great Exterminator.

DOCTOR

I'll do it!

EMPEROR DALEK

Then prove yourself, Doctor. What are you, coward or killer?

DOCTOR

Coward. Any day.[72]

As Tim does in *The Family of Blood*, the Doctor identifies himself here as someone who will always act as a 'coward' rather than take the aggressive position. As we discuss below, this might be a reaction to his recent experiences rather than an expression of his true nature, but he is also placing himself in contrast to both the

---

[71] *Human Nature* [NA] pp241, 247, 268. The phrase was popularised in Dicks, Terrance, and Malcolm Hulke, *The Making of Doctor Who* (1976).
[72] *The Parting of the Ways.*

Daleks and his earlier actions. By the time of the 10th Doctor's involvement in *The Day of the Doctor*, though, he is prompted to return to explicitly rejecting describing himself as a coward:

CLARA

> You told me the name you chose was a promise. What was the promise?

10TH DOCTOR

> Never cruel or cowardly.

WAR DOCTOR

> Never give up, never give in.[73]

But the Doctor is also characterised by his history of running and hiding. For an example of this, we can look to the conversation in *The Sound of Drums* (2007) where he discusses the history of the Master and himself. He claims that when he looked into the Untempered Schism he 'ran away' and 'never stopped', whereas the Master became insane instead. In contrast, the Doctor's more recent history sees him accepting the necessary mantle of soldier, despite it being abhorrent to him, and suffering serious negative consequences that he still grapples with. It is the Master who most recently fled, to escape the Time War: 'I ran... I ran so far. Made myself human so they wouldn't be able to find me. Because I was so scared.'[74]

---

[73] *The Day of the Doctor.*
[74] *The Sound of Drums.*

Just War

The contradiction between the Doctor's rejection of cowardice and his support of it in other contexts is echoed in the shifting emphasis that the episode places on the necessity of war. The headmaster, Rocastle, suggests that the boys are training for warfare which will benefit them and the world: 'I hope, Latimer, that one day you may have a just and proper war in which to prove yourself.'[75]

Many have questioned whether the First World War was indeed a 'just war'[76]. The general question of whether war can be just was a theme throughout the **New Adventures**, even serving as a title for one of them – Lance Parkin's *Just War* (1996).

In *Human Nature* [NA], there is much discussion of whether there is ever a justifiable cause for warfare, and specifically for becoming a soldier who will inevitably cause or suffer death:

> 'Timothy sat down, his legs crossed, on the edge of the rug. "That's what I wanted to ask about. I wanted to ask, don't most soldiers get killed? Especially when there are machine guns involved? Isn't this a bad thing to teach them, in that case?" His blue eyes stared at Smith, who fumbled with his tie awkwardly.
>
> '"Questions like that, they're too big for us..." he muttered.
>
> '"You see, my father said I would be a soldier, but I think that means I shall die. Or worse, that I shall kill other people. I don't want to do it. What should I do?"

[75] *Human Nature* [TV].

[76] Cornell calls the First World War 'genuinely meaningless' in the Authors' Notes to the ebook (*Human Nature* [NA], ebook, p342).

> '"There's a passage in *Henry V* that I could recommend[77]. It's not a sin to kill people if your sovereign's ordered you to do it, because the decisions of war are between him and God. It's not your fault if you're obeying orders."
>
> '"So the murders are his fault?"
>
> '"Well, in war it's not exactly murder. There are bigger things involved. King and country, duty to your fellows. That sort of thing."'[78]

While the novel's John Smith argues that sometimes war is justified, he seems disinclined to participate, and hesitates when asked to actually take part in a direct action against the Aubertides. In contrast, the television Smith, while nominally less pro-war in the sense that he agrees with Joan that war is undesirable, is the one who calls the boys to arms at the start of *The Family of Blood*. In the book, this jingoistic enthusiasm, and that action in the equivalent scene, is exhibited by the headmaster, Mr Rocastle. The choice to give this character's actions to John Smith is an interesting one, given that Rocastle is in neither version a particularly sympathetic figure[79], and thus it potentially paints our leading character in a less flattering light, but is perhaps also more

---

[77] The passage seems to be the central, prose section of Act IV scene 1, where the disguised Henry is talking with his troops, though the viewpoint Smith mentions is only one of those put forward in the discussion.

[78] *Human Nature* [NA] p125.

[79] Though his blimpish tendencies are softened in the novel by his feelings for Joan, and on TV by his ill-fated attempt to rescue 'Lucy Cartwright' from the battlefield.

true to the gung-ho ethos of the 10th Doctor, as discussed in Chapter 1.

It is also worth noting that in the book version, significantly more fatalities are attached to the alien pursuit of the Doctor, despite Joan's accusations in the television version that the Doctor has brought death to the school and village[80]. In the book, the school is destroyed by a nuclear weapon, with several casualties, as well as action by the army who join the combat. Again, some of this may be due to a change in the target audience, with the television story intended to be watched by children as well as adults. There is a limit to the level of unreversed violence and death that can be introduced in such a story. However the book also much more definitively includes the message that war is pointless and undesirable. This is explicit, to some extent, in the coda.

In the book, this includes the elderly Tim Dean wearing not a red poppy, but a white one: a pacifist symbol (though not without its own controversies)[81]. The TV episodes' choice to make Tim a solder in the First World War rather than having a medical role as a member of the Red Cross, means that the messages being sent by the two versions are very different[82]. Despite the anti-war

[80] Though it is unclear how much damage and death results from the missile bombardment by the Family, since we see it onscreen only from a distance.

[81] The white poppy is distributed by the Peace Pledge Union, a pacifist organisation founded prior to World War II, which continues to draw some criticism for its support of appeasement before the war.

[82] As does the Doctor's violent retribution (one might even say revenge) against the Family. See Chapter 4 for further discussion of this.

trappings, the traditional imagery of glorification is upheld by the end, and the symbolism honouring those who fought.

This may also be reflected in, or a consequence of, the sidelining of the plot thread which involves period characters anachronistically learning about the First World War. As discussed in Chapter 1, this is a major part of Benny's story in the novel, and we see reactions to such knowledge of the future from Tim and from Alexander Shuttleworth. But while all seem to accept that war will inevitably come, and assume that the future cannot be changed (especially individual deaths) this is not supported by what actually happens. The fate of individuals, we learn, is not fixed, and should not be assumed as such.

Rather than gaining insight into the future war through burgeoning Time Lord powers and a handy time-based barrier, Tim in the television version has his own psychic powers, remarked on fleetingly by John Smith towards the end of the story when he handles the watch and briefly regains his Doctorly knowledge. This change in agency is possibly linked to the fact that, as noted, the change to the future timeline is under Tim's control (he remembers, prompted by the normal horological functioning of the Doctor's watch, and pushes Hutchinson out of the way of the bomb) rather than a side-effect of the actions which took place[83]. In the novel, despite the fact that Hutchinson does remember the prediction, he is not saved by it, though Hadleman is saved by Tim's presence[84].

---

[83] *The Family of Blood*.
[84] *Human Nature* [NA] pp265-67.

However, the War itself is again seen as being unavoidable, and apparently as something that in some sense **should** not be avoided:

TIM

I just wanted to say goodbye. And thank you. Because I've seen the future and I now know what must be done. It's coming, isn't it? The biggest war ever.

MARTHA

You don't have to fight.

TIM

I think we do.

Though the story pushes against the nostalgic view of the First World War as honourable and necessary, by the end it is being reinforced. Tim concedes that is inevitable to fight, and has 'conquered' his cowardice to play a necessary role in combat, one which results in him being placed to save Hutchinson. Tim becomes a hero, his cowardice perhaps being 'fixed'.

Hollow, Straw Men

Another change between the book and the television episodes sheds a different light on the apparent shift in messages. Much of the uncanny imagery of the Family is brought across from the book versions of the characters: the little girl with the red balloon, the idea that they are following the 'scent' of the Doctor, and their use of familial terms for each other[85]. But one addition for the

[85] Though this is more foregrounded in the TV version, as discussed in Chapter 3.

television series is the army they create to fight their battle, with a shape stolen from the scarecrow that guards a nearby field[86]. As 'Baines' describes their creation: 'Molecular fringe animation fashioned in the shape of straw men. My own private army, sir. It's ever so good, sir.'[87]

While 'straw men' may be a valid literal description of the creatures, it is also a term that will be familiar to anyone versed in rhetorical models (or perhaps who has engaged in any protracted arguments in online forums). A straw man is a type of logical fallacy, an argumentative debate tactic that is flawed. It involves one person in the debate arguing against something that is similar to, but not the same as, the original argument put forward by their opponent; by finding a convincing counter-argument they may appear to have won, and congratulate themselves on having done so, but this is not the case. To build a straw man is to fight something pointlessly, that does not really exist and obscures the real threat. This idea has analogies in the episode itself, both in terms of the scarecrows as an invulnerable distraction from the Family, and the idea that it is the willingness to wage battle that is the threat to the schoolboys, not their nominal opponents. This, again, may be related to the scene at the school firing range. The identification of the imaginary opponents as 'tribesmen from the dark continent' sets them up as a terrifying, savage Other, but 'They only have spears' is both a reason not to be afraid to attack,

---

[86] Cornell notes that Russell T Davies suggested the idea of the scarecrows, in response to the perception that a 'monster' was needed in addition to the human-shaped Family. ('Adapting the Novel for the Screen', p360).

[87] *The Family of Blood*.

and Tim's explanation for why he should not do so [88]. In either case, the opponent as perceived does not truly exist.

Elsewhere, the scarecrows are referred to as 'soldiers'. There is yet another important reference that we can take from the men of straw, and that is to TS Eliot's poem 'The Hollow Men'[89]. The poem, which along with the eponymous subjects references scarecrows and speaks of a 'Headpiece filled with straw'[90], has many interpretations but as with much of Eliot's poetry is often associated with war themes. It was written in the period following the First World War, and some believe it to be commentary on post-War Europe[91].

The poem, which makes reference to Joseph Conrad's *Heart of Darkness* (1899)[92] (also concerned with 'savages'), was famously used in the similarly inspired *Apocalypse Now* (1979), a film which does not conform to the romantic idealisation of war described above but highlights its brutality, meaninglessness and propensity to destroy men. Eliot himself struggled with the complexity of whether the necessity of war could ever justify the cost in suffering that would result. This included arguing against the pacifist AA Milne, to garner the response: 'Mr Eliot's thoughts on war give nobody any clues as to what he really thinks about it [...] I do not

---

[88] *Human Nature* [TV].
[89] Originally published in Eliot, TS, *Poems: 1909-1925*.
[90] Eliot, TS, *The Complete Poems and Plays of TS Eliot*, p83.
[91] Krockel, Carl, *War Trauma and English Modernism: TS Eliot and DH Lawrence*.
[92] Eliot, *The Complete Poems and Plays*, p81.

even know if he would be glad to wake tomorrow into a warless world.'[93]

By referring to the scarecrows as his army, 'Baines' recalls the notion of the disposable solider, whose individuality and welfare do not matter and who are there purely as fodder for the conflict. While it could be suggested that the militarisation inherent in creating an army does not seem to mesh well with the Family's ethos of relying on their own small unit against the world, it echoes the patriotic jingoism of protecting the 'family' of one's country by creating these disposable soldiers. We should consider whether some of the arguments being presented by the Family regarding war and conflict are also 'straw men', and are false equivalences. This ties in to the themes of 'just war' described above, in that the Family force Smith to make a false choice between giving them the watch and facilitating war, or destroying himself and the ones he loves. But he finds a third choice – albeit one which is also destructive to his identity as John Smith, and his relationship with Joan, rather than causing literal death.

Effects of Trauma

If we accept that these episodes contain, at least in part, an anti-war narrative, then it is also important to consider how this fits into the wider story being told. As mentioned above, military conflict is not an unusual topic for **Doctor Who.** The story of the Doctor in 21st-century **Doctor Who** in particular can be read in its entirely as one of the result of conflict, war and trauma. Though it can be awkward to 'diagnose' a fictional character in this way, an analysis by psychologists has suggested that the Doctor meets several of

[93] Cited in Krockel, *War Trauma and English Modernism*, p157.

the criteria for someone suffering from a form of post-traumatic stress disorder (PTSD)[94]. This episode, and the season as a whole, highlight that experiences of warfare are not outside the scope of **Doctor Who** and remind us that this is a character who has lost everything through conflict, and is profoundly affected by it.

While *Human Nature / The Family of Blood* has a focus on the effects of war, this has been a recurring theme throughout the preceding 21st-century series. Significantly, both of the occasions mentioned earlier when the Doctor, seemingly counter to his stated views on weapons, wields (and contemplates using) a gun, occur when he discovers that one of the civilisations he believed he made extinct has in fact survived the Time War. It may well be that the extremity of his reaction to weapons during this time is at least partly the result of such trauma.

The actions of the ninth Doctor in particular, with his avoidance behaviour and violent outbursts[95], seem to show us clearly that the regenerations which take place following the Time War result in a character suffering extreme trauma and guilt. As Janina Scarlet and Alan Kistler put it:

> 'When the Doctor experiences that rage and avoids talking about his experiences, he may be struggling with at least some symptoms of PTSD. His experiences are similar to what many combat veterans undergo after exposure to battle.

[94] Erickson, Kristen, and Matt Munson, with Stephen Prescott and Travis Langley, 'Post-Time War Stress Disorder'. Langley, Travis, ed, *Doctor Who Psychology: A Madman with a Box* (2016).
[95] Erickson et al find these in *The End of the World* (2005) and *Dalek* respectively ('Post-Time War Stress Disorder', pp192-93, 196).

> This is especially true when it comes to anger and aggression when encountering a reminder of the war (a Dalek, for example).'[96]

The impression given by the ninth Doctor is of a character who is repressing a traumatic experience and avoiding discussion of it, while being clearly impacted by it, and trying to deal with the relatively recent events. The first place he takes Rose after meeting her is to the destruction of her planet, and this acts as a catalyst for him to express to her that his is gone.

DOCTOR

> You think it'll last forever, people and cars and concrete, but it won't. One day it's all gone, even the sky. My planet's gone. It's dead. It burned like the Earth. It's just rocks and dust before its time.

ROSE

> What happened?

DOCTOR

> There was a war and we lost.[97]

The phrasing of this, given what we learn later, is interesting; technically speaking the Time War could be said to have been a stalemate or pyrrhic victory, but as the Doctor clarifies later in *Dalek*, he considers that 'everyone lost'. He also, however,

---

[96] Scarlet, Janina, and Alan Kistler, 'The Compassionate Doctor: Caring for Self by Caring for Others', p22. Langley, ed, *Doctor Who Psychology*.
[97] *The End of the World*.

contradicts himself in the very same episode: 'I'm the only one left. I win. How about that?'

We see an uncharacteristically vicious outburst from the Doctor in this episode against the eponymous Dalek; he insists it should die, and does not seem to exhibit any of his customary compassion. This reaction provides the first real glimpse of how the experiences the Doctor has had may be affecting his character. This emerges further as the series continues, but it is already clear that his status as the last survivor is a very important part of his current worldview.

DOCTOR

I couldn't... I wasn't... Oh, Rose. They're all dead.

DALEK

Why do we survive?

DOCTOR

I don't know.[98]

This exchange reinforces the notion that the Doctor is experiencing some form of survivor's guilt, in that he alone emerged unscathed from the War. The final episodes of the 2005 season could be seen as a form of cathartic release of some of his guilt. He is asked to make the same choice again – to destroy every living thing present, including the Daleks, but also all of Earth. But he does not. As quoted at the start of this chapter, he chooses to be a 'coward', identifying himself as such in the same way Tim does, rather than repeat his earlier regretted actions. It is Rose who 'ends' the Time

[98] *Dalek*.

War on his behalf, and destroys the Daleks, and the Doctor saves her by himself dying. In his final words before regenerating, he acknowledges that he was 'fantastic'; perhaps purged of some of his guilt over his previous actions, he is proud of how he behaved this time around[99].

Following his regeneration, in contrast to the sometimes moody and taciturn ninth Doctor, the 10th Doctor is frequently exuberant, and almost manic. This, however may be a different form of denial; he has lost some of his guilt, but still feels deep grief about the loss of his home. This behaviour, then could be seen as repression, to divert himself from thinking about the trauma by throwing himself as hard as possible into other activities. This works for a while, but with the loss of Rose at the end of the second series, the façade begins to break down. The 10th Doctor, while on the surface appearing to be charismatic, joyful and curious, does also sometimes show behaviours which might be considered out of character for that persona; for one, his somewhat callous refusal to acknowledge or deal with Martha's feelings for him, which he does seem at some level to be aware of[100].

The theme of how past military experience carries through and affects the Doctor in his current life is one that continues onward into regenerations after the 10th. The 11th Doctor, while on the surface more carefree and unaffected by his past, has a different conflict at the heart of his story; not the Time War, but echoes of a war in his future, the battle at Trenzalore that seems to be the inescapable end of his life. In *A Good Man Goes to War* (2011), he

---

[99] *The Parting of the Ways*.
[100] See *The Shakespeare Code* in particular.

learns that his name is in some places synonymous with the word for a warrior, and the remainder of his tenure includes him coming to terms with this inevitability. However, it is not until *The Day of the Doctor* that he truly can reconcile with his past; in part because he learns that he did **not** do what he has previously been unable to accept. This journey that the character has travelled is made explicit by the Moment's 'Bad Wolf' interface as she addresses him at the point of his decision, and describes the 10th and 11th Doctors: 'They're you. They're what you become if you destroy Gallifrey. The man who regrets and the man who forgets.'[101]

We do not learn how she would describe the ninth Doctor, but perhaps he would be the man who grieves. At the end of *The Time of the Doctor*, with the continued existence of Gallifrey confirmed, though it is supposedly locked away forever, we might expect the 12th Doctor to be the man who healed.

Returning to *Human Nature / The Family of Blood*, and fitting it within this schema, we can look at how Martha talks to Joan about how John Smith is more than he appears at first sight:

MARTHA

> But it's deeper than that. Sometimes when you look in his eyes you know, you just know that there's something else in there. Something hidden. Right behind the eyes, something hidden away in the dark.[102]

This could be read simply as a reference to the Doctor's hidden nature as an ancient alien being, but the fact that this other self is

---

[101] *The Day of the Doctor.*
[102] *Human Nature* [TV].

hidden 'behind the eyes' is perhaps also a reflection on how the Doctor hides his internal conflict and sadness resulting from his great age and experience, and in particular his part in the War. Eliot's 'The Hollow Men', referenced earlier in relation to its men of straw, also has a recurring motif of eyes, and what they might reveal or conceal: 'Eyes I dare not meet in dreams'[103]. Martha's perception of hidden things being recognisable by looking in the eyes of another has resonance with descriptions of those who have suffered trauma. This recurrent motif is referred to by *TV Tropes* as the 'Thousand-Yard Stare', a term which originated during the First World War to refer to the apparent distance the lack of near-focus in such a look might imply, but was popularised in 1945 via a painting by Tom Lea in *Life* magazine[104]. Such an empty, frozen look is often used as a cue for how traumatised veterans can be recognised, both in fiction and journalism, and in media a focus on the eyes is often used as a shorthand for those whose experiences give an inner, unknowable distance[105].

In *Human Nature* [NA], the Doctor's reaction to a difficult emotional period is to put himself away, creating a new persona

---

[103] Eliot, *The Complete Poems and Plays*, p83.

[104] The painting, subsequently titled *Marines Call It That 2,000 Yard Stare*, is a common point of visual reference in war-related media. For example, in *Serenity*, the intended first episode of **Firefly** (2002), Captain Malcolm Reynolds, having been ordered to surrender, watches departing air support with his eyes framed in a manner deliberately echoing it to the extent that (as referenced in the DVD episode commentary) his blinks were digitally erased.

[105] Examples of this are many and varied, particularly in media portraying war, from the 1980 episode of **M*A*S*H** (1972-83) *Heal Thyself* to films such as *Full Metal Jacket* (1987).

that can potentially be unaffected by this history of violence and war. While the television equivalent is a more direct withdrawal from violence, the notion of retreat replacing engagement is still there, if somewhat more subtle. The Doctor's reaction when the pretence is lifted is to insist that it makes no difference, but this is not true; he cannot remain the innocent John Smith, with no awareness of the wider context and of who he really is.

Like the shadow of Trenzalore in his future which hangs over the 11th Doctor, and the contemporary characters in *Human Nature / The Family of Blood* who cannot divert from a course which will bring them to the First World War, the Doctor must accept that some things are inevitable and inescapable. However the choices that he makes, as both Smith and the Doctor, can be looked at in terms of sacrifice despite, to some extent, a lack of choice. This fits into the broader themes that we will look at in more detail in Chapter 4.

CHAPTER 3: SCHOOL AND FAMILY

Despite being primarily intended for a young audience, throughout much of its existence **Doctor Who** rarely featured child characters, and it was equally rare for it to show much interest in the day-to-day lives of children. Although the very first episode of the series is set partly in a school and deals with a family relationship – establishing links of family and pedagogy which would continue to bind the original quartet of regulars[106] – during the rest of 20th-century **Doctor Who** families were rarely prominent, and schools a setting hardly ever visited. In these terms, *Human Nature / The Family of Blood* – dealing as it does with a school under attack from a family – is clearly an outlier.

Interestingly, though, both these absences have been filled during the 21st century, by successive showrunners. Russell T Davies embraced family relationships within the series' drama, bringing relatives particularly to the fore in his companions' backstories and present conflicts, while Steven Moffat would make more extensive use of school settings in 2013-16 than all of his predecessors, as well as increasing the prevalence of child characters.

By one measure, Davies' family-saga approach to **Doctor Who** reaches its zenith in the 2007 season: Martha Jones brings with her more relatives than any other companion, of any era. Her mother Francine, sister Tish, brother Leo (with his girlfriend Shonara and daughter Keisha) and father Clive (with his own girlfriend Annalise) appear in variously significant roles in five of the season's 13

---

[106] 'An Unearthly Child' (*An Unearthly Child* episode 1, 1963). Susan is the Doctor's granddaughter, and Ian and Barbara are her teachers.

episodes[107]. Cornell, too, has history in this respect: his earlier TV story, *Father's Day*, made a major contribution to the development of Rose's family, introducing (then killing off) her father Pete, whose alternative-history equivalent became a recurring character during the following season[108].

In stories of this era, families are often significant even when the companions' own relatives are absent. In the 2007 season, only *Daleks in Manhattan / Evolution of the Daleks* is lacking significant reference to biological relationship[109]. Only in the three years (1987-89) when Andrew Cartmel was Script Editor had there been anything like as strong a focus on families[110] – although the fact

---

[107] Specifically *Smith and Jones, The Lazarus Experiment, 42, The Sound of Drums* and *Last of the Time Lords* (all 2007). Francine later returns in *The Stolen Earth / Journey's End* (2008). Martha's cousin Adeola previously appeared in *Army of Ghosts*, but as this relationship is largely a post hoc explanation for why both parts are played by Freema Agyeman it seems excessive to count it here.

[108] In *Rise of the Cybermen / The Age of Steel* and *Army of Ghosts / Doomsday* (all 2006).

[109] Other than the appearances of Martha's family, in *The Shakespeare Code*, the youngest of the three Carrionites in Elizabethan London calls her compatriots 'my mothers'; in *Gridlock*, Thomas and Valerie Brannigan are biological parents to a litter of kittens; in *Blink*, Kathy Nightingale has a brother and acquires a grandson; in *Utopia*, Padra Shafe Cane is reunited with his mother and brother.

[110] Family relationships between the characters feature in *Time and the Rani, Delta and the Bannermen* and *Dragonfire* (all 1987), *Remembrance of the Daleks* (1988) and all four stories of the 1989 season (including *The Curse of Fenric*, which introduces Ace's mother and grandmother, and addresses in passing the death of her grandfather).

that this was, in 2005, the most recent regularly broadcast version of the series, perhaps suggests that Davies' reinvention of the formula was less radical in this area than is often supposed.

By contrast, other than that very first episode, only three TV stories prior to *Human Nature / The Family of Blood* are set even partially in places identifiable as schools[111]. Of these, arguably only the previous year's *School Reunion* (2006) makes full use of the setting, integrating the drama with the routine life of the school, its teachers, pupils and ancillary staff[112]. 'An Unearthly Child' (1963) includes brief classroom scenes, but is largely about the extracurricular obsession of two teachers with a particular pupil; similarly *Remembrance of the Daleks* (1988) includes a pupil and a headmaster as characters, but shows us little of their institutional life beyond an empty classroom. In fact Coal Hill School's real function in the latter story, like that of IM Foreman's junkyard, is to evoke nostalgia by revisiting the settings of the former[113].

Controlling Our Boarders

Both Coal Hill and *School Reunion*'s Deffry Vale School are state schools, however – a quite different setting from an independent

---

[111] Others, such as *The Time Monster* (1972) or *Shada*, are set partially in universities or research institutions, but these would not normally be classified as 'schools' in British English.

[112] Notably, Rose is installed as a dinner lady while the Doctor teaches – compare this with the respective statuses of Martha and Smith in *Human Nature / The Family of Blood*.

[113] The present-day Coal Hill School would reappear for similar reasons in *The Day of the Doctor*, but would be revisited extensively in 2014 and 2015 as Clara's workplace, eventually becoming the setting of 21st-century **Doctor Who**'s third spinoff series, **Class** (2016).

boys' boarding-school like Farringham School for Boys in *Human Nature / The Family of Blood*. The latter category – known confusingly and for tedious historical reasons as 'public schools' – have historically been cornerstones of British cultural identity, despite the fact that only a tiny percentage of the population attend them. Their tradition of selection on social and financial grounds has meant that for centuries they were (and have not yet ceased to be) largely responsible for educating the UK's aristocratic, political, ecclesiastical and military officer classes, as well as a sizeable minority of those in the former British colonies.

Though *Human Nature / The Family of Blood* is in no way wrong in suggesting that many of Farringham's pupils in 1913 would have ended up dead on First World War battlefields, they would have served as commissioned officers, not enlisted men. Not old enough to have made strategic decisions leading to the deaths of thousands of working-class soldiers (nor to have enjoyed the protection from direct combat of the senior officers who did), it would have been they and their peers who led those soldiers to their deaths.

In fiction, boys' boarding-schools are often liminal spaces, whose primary occupants are on the cusp between childhood and adulthood[114]. Treated in some respects as adults while being deprived of basic autonomy in others, the pupils act out harsh and macho fantasies of manhood not dissimilar to those in William

---

[114] Although the increasingly democratic sympathies of TV audiences mean that boarding-schools have not generally been a popular setting for TV drama in the 21st century. On the DVD commentary for *The Family of Blood*, composer Murray Gold calls them 'a don't-go-to territory' which 'nobody wants to see.'

Golding's *Lord of the Flies* (1954). Although in reality such schools' characters vary widely, and in recent decades many reforms have been made, they remain a byword among the British populace at large for institutionalised bullying, 'fagging' (the practice of making younger boys act as servants to older ones) and expedient, often abusive, same-sex relationships. While there is little hint of the third of these, the other two are clearly present in the scene in *Human Nature* [TV] which introduces Tim, Baines and Hutchinson – though the bullying Tim experiences is far more severe in the source novel.

Doctor Who's sole prior excursion into similar territory was *Mawdryn Undead* (1983) – coincidentally a story in which a regular character is found suffering from amnesia and working as a teacher at a boarding-school, one of whose pupils is a scheming extraterrestrial, and which culminates with the Doctor deciding reluctantly to sacrifice himself to defuse a threat posed by a group of aliens plotting to steal his life force. Though it was made 24 years before *Human Nature / The Family of Blood*, and is set 70 (and also 64) years after it, *Mawdryn Undead* portrays a closely similar establishment with all the traditional elements: a grandiose rural setting, a gowned headmaster, male teachers, a matron, a cadet corps, and abusive power dynamics within the student body. Despite the broad similarities, however, major elements of *Mawdryn Undead* – the dual time-scheme with its mildly farcical plot dynamics, the 'reunion' element added by the reappearance of the Brigadier, and the Faustian bargain made by the Doctor's new companion Turlough – have no clear equivalents in *Human Nature / The Family of Blood*. The many differences in detail make it difficult to consider it a primary influence, and neither the book nor Cornell's supplementary material mention it as such.

More significant, perhaps, may be two books set in public schools – or perhaps more relevantly their adaptations by the BBC in the early 1980s, whose connections to **Doctor Who** might cause a diligent fan to seek either of them out. *To Serve Them All My Days*, a 1972 novel by RF Delderfield, deals with a traumatised history teacher after the First World War who falls in love with a nurse, and whose anti-war stance puts him at odds with the overt militarism of his colleagues; it ends with adumbrations of the coming Second World War, in which many more of the school's pupils are likely to lose their lives. The BBC broadcast an adaptation in 1980-81, featuring Matthew Waterhouse (who also played the Doctor's companion Adric) in a supporting role. *Goodbye, Mr Chips* (1934) is a novella by James Hilton, adapted by the BBC in 1984 as a miniseries sharing a producer (Barry Letts), script editor (Terrance Dicks) and incidental music composer (Dudley Simpson) with early-1970s **Doctor Who**. It likewise considers the effect of the First World War on a minor public school, and ends with premonitions of the Second. On his deathbed, the titular unmarried schoolmaster speaks sentimentally of his 'children', meaning the boys he has taught.

Rather clearer lines of influence connect the story with Lindsay Anderson's politically subversive film *If....* (1968), which *Doctor Who: The Discontinuity Guide* (1995), co-authored by Cornell, cites as a possible source for *Mawdryn Undead*[115]. *If....*'s public-school

[115] Cornell, Paul, Martin Day and Keith Topping, *Doctor Who: The Discontinuity Guide*, p286.

setting features a similarly militarised and hierarchical discipline to that of Farringham, with boys trained in machine-gun technique and sanctioned punishment beatings administered by the head boy, Barnes (whose name recalls that of Baines). Like *Human Nature / The Family of Blood*, the film makes use of the hymn 'To Be a Pilgrim', and it culminates with the breakdown of the school order, involving a gun battle which is ironically juxtaposed with a hymn tune.

In *If....*, the school stands for a microcosm of society at large, and as such it becomes the target of an armed revolutionary uprising[116]. *Human Nature / The Family of Blood* finds a further use for this parallel, as a cue to make the school the venue for what **Doctor Who** scholarship has traditionally categorised as a 'Base Under Siege' story – a stock plot where a small group of human beings in an isolated location must use their finite resources to defend themselves against an army of monsters. This was a formula refined to the point of inevitability during Patrick Troughton's tenure as the Doctor (1966-69), and frequently revisited since: familiar secondary elements include a weak leader, misguided attempts to broker peace with the invaders, dissent in the ranks and an infiltrator within the walls, all of which *Human Nature / The Family of Blood* reproduces. Indeed, the main element lacking from

---

[116] The extreme stability and durability of the public school as an institution is shown – even in the face of such escapist fantasy – by the fact that the settings of the various works cited here cover well over a century, from 1870 (when 'Mr Chips' begins teaching) to 1983, taking in the First and Second World Wars and the revolutionary fervour of Anderson's 1960s with little apparent change.

the standard scenario is the Doctor, which may be why this 'base' falls so spectacularly, leaving its occupants to flee.

This microcosmic mirroring of external society is an outcome of the geographical isolation of such bases, shared by many boarding-schools. Perhaps the single most important distinction between these institutions and state schools like Coal Hill is that the former remove their students from the moderating influence of their families. This is fitting, because in *Human Nature / The Family of Blood*, the preoccupation of Davies-era **Doctor Who** with family is expressed primarily in negative terms, with families – other than the story's antagonists – appearing mostly as a series of gaps in the narrative.

Families, Absent and Alien

Although evidence of human families is everywhere in the story, blood relationships other than those of the eponymous Family are conspicuously absent. Hutchinson's father and Tim's uncle are mentioned, but both have had or will soon have postings in Africa, and are present only in memory or by correspondence. Another boy, Jenkins, is said to be 'missing his mother'[117]. Martha is cut off from her own extensive support network of relatives, and unlike Benny in *Human Nature* [NA] she cannot even pose as Smith's niece. Young Lucy Cartwright has parents, but by the time we learn of their existence they have been 'vanished' by her replacement: when we see their family home, it is significantly empty[118].

---

[117] *Human Nature* [TV].
[118] *The Family of Blood*.

The family Smith remembers is entirely fictional[119], and he lacks any emotional connection with his memories of them. Joan's marriage to Oliver was childless, and although she and Smith have children in the flashforward sequence, after its events are averted they, too, become haunting absences. (We will learn in *The End of Time* (2009-10) that Joan had descendants, having evidently remarried later, but that falls outside the scope of this story[120].) The elderly Tim in the present-day coda is seemingly accompanied by a much younger man who, in contrast to most of those present, is not in military uniform, but unlike in the novel there is nothing to confirm that this is a family member rather than a friend or professional carer.

Thus positive depictions of family are relegated to the margins of the story, while the Family who take centre stage are the story's eponymous villains. Two years earlier, in *Aliens of London / World War Three* (2005), the idea of a family of monsters was considered sufficiently innovative to be couched as a plot revelation:

DOCTOR

Then something's brought the Slitheen race here. What is it?

SLITHEEN / GENERAL ASQUITH

'The Slitheen race'?

---

[119] A point that is reinforced by the metafictional fact of his parents being named after two real figures in the early history of **Doctor Who**, Verity Lambert and Sidney Newman (*Human Nature* [TV]).
[120] *The End of Time* episode 2 (2010).

SLITHEEN / JOSEPH GREEN

Slitheen is not our species. Slitheen is our surname.[121]

Certainly this is something of a departure from previous **Doctor Who**, where non-human families have tended to belong to sympathetic or morally complex species – such as Delta and her daughter in *Delta and the Bannermen* (1987), or the Draconian Emperor and Prince in *Frontier in Space* (1973). The exceptions are those species (often with only one speaking individual, for reasons of either biology or production budget) that explicitly reproduce but are not presented in terms of 'family' – such as the Wirrn in *The Ark in Space* (1975) or the Gastropods in *The Twin Dilemma* (1984). The Slitheen do seem – at least in *Aliens of London / World War Three* (though one of their number later receives some moral shading in *Boom Town* (2005)) – to be the series' first group of thoroughgoing monsters whose explicit allegiance is to a common family rather than a species[122].

Though only the third such monstrous family (after the Carrionites[123]), the Family of Blood take this motif to an extreme, in

---

[121] *World War Three*. This is the dialogue as delivered in the episode, which is assigned differently from that in Davies, Russell T, et al, *Doctor Who: The Shooting Scripts* (2005), p171.

[122] Two partial precedents are perhaps the Foamasi in *The Leisure Hive* (1980), who belong to a criminal fraternity (which in human culture – especially that of the Mafiosi of whom they are anagrams – might also mean a family), and the Androgums in *The Two Doctors* (1985), who owe clan allegiances (though not to the same clan).

[123] The cat-nuns and Krillitanes use the titles 'sister' and 'brother' (*New Earth* (2006), *School Reunion*), but without any clear indication of the corresponding relationships. Mother Bloodtide

that the fact of their relationship defines them almost exclusively. We know a few facts about them – they are predatory, hunting by scent; they have ephemeral lifespans; they are shapeshifters, who seem to exist in a gaseous state between bodies – but in terms of identity they are effectively anonymous. Compared with their equivalents in *Human Nature* [NA] – who are given well-defined individual personalities on top of personal names, a family name, a species name and a named home planet[124] – they are stripped of virtually all defining features. In their case, it is not the family that is a significant absence, but everything other than the Family.

Their personalities are not clearly distinguished from one another. Their species and planet of origin are never even referred to. Their group identifier, 'The Family of Blood', sounds sufficiently specific to be a name – 'Blood' can be a surname in English, after all – but could simply mean that they are a biological family, related by blood. As individuals, they are called either by the names they steal from those they mimic ('Jenny', 'Baines', 'Lucy Cartwright', 'Mr Clark'), or by relationship markers ('Mother of Mine', 'Son of Mine' and so on – when one is addressing all the rest, 'Family of Mine')[125]. These are not equivalent to names as English speakers understand

---

also addresses the captive Carrionite horde as 'sisters', but the verbal evidence of family relationships among the Carrionites is stronger: Lilith's form of address is not merely 'mother' but 'my mothers', and she refers to Mother Bloodtide and Mother Doomfinger as her 'parents'.

[124] They are August, Greeneye, Laylock, Serif, Aphasia and Hoff, of the family Dubraxine, and they are Aubertides from the planet Aubis (*Human Nature* [NA] pp10-12, 128, 163).

[125] Cornell credits this idea to Russell T Davies (*Human Nature* [TV] DVD commentary).

them, as they vary according to who is addressing the individual: for instance, 'Lucy' is called 'Daughter of Mine' by 'Jenny', but 'Sister of Mine' by 'Baines'. Such identifiers could not, by definition, be used by individuals outside the Family.

This suggestion of an alternative system of nomenclature is unusually inventive for **Doctor Who**, where aliens are more usually given invented names which function like personal names (frequently mononyms), but it hints at two possible further implications. Firstly, that these shapeshifters may spend so much of their lives under assumed personas that they see no value in having identities of their own. Secondly, that family would very likely be more important than individuality in the worldview of a species whose individuals are short-lived but whose families will, presumably, persist from one generation to the next[126].

This correlates with the fact that the Family members are hardly demonstrative in their affection for one another. Their interactions together lack the cruelty and rapaciousness they show in dealing with outsiders, they share a common purpose ('We wanted to live forever'), and they respond with concern when one of their number is threatened; yet they express scant feeling for one another, and are capable of, for instance, sending their ostensibly youngest and most vulnerable member into enemy territory for utilitarian tactical reasons[127]. Again, we might suppose that a species which places low value on the individual would make

---

[126] Although this does raise a further question, for discussion of which see Appendix 2.
[127] *The Family of Blood*.

relatively little of personal relationships: the family as a whole would be the object of any available devotion.

This particular Family, though, would appear to be dissidents from that tradition. While displaying these presumable cultural norms of their species, they evidently value their own existence as individuals, hence their quest for extended life. This aligns their motivations with those of the Aubertides of *Human Nature* [NA], who want access to Time Lord biology to overcome the restrictions on their reproductive potential[128]. In both cases the villains' driving motivation is to allow their family to transcend their species, elevating a limited clan loyalty over a wider civilisational one.

Growing Up

Given its subject-matter, *Human Nature / The Family of Blood* could have chosen to compare rival social models of child-rearing – the nurturing familial environment versus the challenging scholastic domain – but in practice, this is not a major interest of the story. John Smith, the plot's focus, may have no real family, but nor is he convincingly representative of the school where he teaches, and the character-defining choices he must make are not between these alternatives. The swaggering arrogance of a public schoolboy such as Baines derives as much from confidence in his own family – and therefore class – background as from his educational establishment, and changes little when he is assimilated into the invading alien brood (though Harry Lloyd's twin performances are distinguished in other effective ways).

[128] *Human Nature* [NA] pp129-31.

With the story conspicuously lacking in positive models of family, and the school also an alien environment to the majority of the audience, one is thus left with the sense that the two options have little to choose between them. In the end, the conflict of Farringham school versus the Family of Blood is not a thematic one between abstract principles, but a plot-based one between two specific, and manifestly imperfect, social groups.

From it, though, emerges a small support network, which is derived from school connections but functions in other ways like a family. Smith, Joan, Martha and Tim are all formally associated with Farringham School, in distinct roles as teacher, nurse, maid and student, but their connections are not derived from these functions. Smith and Joan, who the flashforward suggests would otherwise have become a mother and father, are joined by romantic love; Martha is Smith's platonic friend; and all three stand as older protectors to Tim. From a certain angle they might look like parents, a child and his aunt, and the Cartwrights' cottage like the family home it used to be before the violent irruption of the false 'Lucy'. In opposing the Family and fleeing the school, these four become something that is neither a biological family nor a school class, but which can fulfil the most basic function of each: the protection of the young.

However, the story's interest is less in rival childhood environments than in outgrowing them – and, generally, in the process of 'growing up' which continues well into adulthood. Tim's farewell scene with the Doctor and Martha reveals that he has decided – against his own earlier pacifist reluctance and Martha's current advice – to fight in the coming War. Though his choice might be seen as retrograde[129], it is one he is making independently for himself, and despite their misgivings Martha and the Doctor respect this, the Doctor going so far as to pass his pocket-watch on to him like an heirloom. Though Thomas Sangster's performance, which portrays Tim as an unusually mature adolescent throughout, tends to obscure this turning-point, in rejecting his own wants in favour of a sense of duty Tim is demonstrating that he has understood what adulthood entails.

The same can be said of Martha, as she takes control of events in the Doctor's absence, and of both Smith and Joan, as they come to understand that their relationship must end. Though their love-affair is certainly not a childish thing, they too must sacrifice their own desires for the sake of the greater good.

In the following scenes we see the older Tim risking his life to save his erstwhile bully, Hutchinson, and then reaching what may be the end of his life, the best part of a century later[130]. Beyond the confines of the story – but not of the arc in which it lies – Martha will come to a similar realisation by the end of the season, as she decides that her need to travel in the TARDIS is outweighed by her duty of care to her own family (and in the longer term to the patients she will treat as a doctor)[131]. Even the Doctor will eventually set aside his plea that 'I don't want to go,' and make way

---

[129] Particularly, as we have seen, by readers of *Human Nature* [NA].
[130] *The Family of Blood*. In the novel, the scene explicitly represents his final waking moments (*Human Nature* [NA] p269).
[131] *Last of the Time Lords*.

for his 11th incarnation – though not before taking steps to find out what happened to Joan in his absence[132].

This maturity is contrasted with the obduracy with which the Family of Blood cling to life, despite early death being part of the natural order for their species. Whereas the others, most obviously Smith and Tim, are prepared not only to step across the threshold into a new phase of their lives but to risk death in doing so, the members of the Family cling to their current existences at the expense of the lives of others. The fittingness of unwanted forms of immortality being their punishment is almost didactic, as if the Doctor is fulfilling the function of a teacher to them – the profession Smith has just definitively abandoned. It may not be a deliberate irony, but it fits the general tone of this cathartic sequence, that the Family end the story by being 'schooled'.

[132] *The End of Time* episode 2.

CHAPTER 4: HUMANITY AND DIVINITY

> 'Of course, the story of an immortal becoming human is older than that Christopher Reeve movie, as old as belief itself.'
>
> [Paul Cornell, 'Introduction', *Human Nature* [NA]][133]
>
> 'God, you're rubbish as a human.'
>
> [Martha, *The Family of Blood*]

In Paul Cornell's first televised **Doctor Who** story, *Father's Day*, an ordinary man is faced with the horrifying necessity of sacrificing his life to save the world. The monsters are attacking, the Doctor has vanished, and in his absence the responsibility for salvation lies in the hands of this flawed, limited man. Terrified of dying and preferring passionately to live, he nonetheless surrenders himself to death, to save those he loves and those he will never meet.

It is a tribute to Cornell's skills as a screenwriter, and Russell T Davies' as a script-editor, that *Human Nature / The Family of Blood*, to which this brief precis equally applies, never feels like a rerun of *Father's Day*. Nor indeed does *Father's Day* feel to readers of the **New Adventures** like a revisitation of *Human Nature* [NA], which also follows the pattern. It is apparent, though, that the theme of self-sacrifice is one that Cornell takes more of an interest in, and treats with more seriousness, than most **Doctor Who** scriptwriters.

---

[133] *Human Nature* [NA] pv.

Sacrificing Selves and Others

Traditionally in **Doctor Who**, self-sacrifice is a plot point rather than a theme: time and again, a one-off character with no long-term role in the series accepts death in order to allow the regulars a victory. With very few exceptions (such as Sara Kingdom's in *The Daleks' Master Plan* (1965-66)), the emotional impact of their deaths is confined to the story in which they appear; in terms of the cost to the Doctor, these characters are small change. (As a general rule, in the 20th century such sacrifices tend to be foregrounded and happen at the climax of their story, while in the 21st century they are often intermediate plot beats buying the Doctor time[134]. Closer reflection, though, may remind us that many nameless soldiers and other non-speaking extras fulfil the latter function in 20th-century stories; the innovation of the 2000s is to characterise them at all.) On the whole, 21st-century **Doctor Who** has tried to give the characters who take such final steps a dignity and a depth of motivation which their 20th-century counterparts often lacked, but very few of them become the focus of their stories in the way that Pete Tyler and John Smith are.

Human Nature [NA] was not the first of Cornell's novels to question the morality of this convention. In *Love and War* the Doctor – portrayed throughout the **New Adventures** as a chess master, playing for high stakes but often forced to improvise after his strategies go awry – faces the emotional fallout after he

---

[134] For example: Lesterson in *The Power of the Daleks* (1966), Galloway in *Death to the Daleks* (1974) and Orcini in *Revelation of the Daleks* (1985) are of the former type; De Maggio in *Dalek* and Gretchen in *Into the Dalek* (2014) belong to the latter. This trope is especially prevalent in Dalek stories.

manoeuvres Ace's new lover, Jan, into a position to sacrifice himself for the common good[135]. The reader is implicitly invited to consider from a new perspective the regular acts of heroic self-sacrifice by others which aid the Doctor; that of those in whose lives – like those of Ace, Rose Tyler and Joan Redfern – the throwaway hero of the week is a loved and irreplaceable presence.

But Cornell's first **Doctor Who** novel – also his first professionally published long-form work – presents self-sacrifice in a more intriguing light. *Timewyrm: Revelation* (1991) draws on Norse myth, Jungian psychoanalysis and early-90s cyberpunk SF to depict the seventh Doctor's psyche as a mindscape in which his past selves and dead acquaintances play various archetypal roles. Ace enters into this virtual realm and, during the novel's climactic sequence, discovers an avatar of the fifth Doctor, wounded and tied to a gigantic tree from which she frees him. He explains that he has been imprisoned here by the currently dominant persona, the seventh Doctor:

> '"I wanted a place to play cricket, you see, a sunny glade and a pot of tea, but he wouldn't let me. We were at war, he said." The old Doctor's voice was full of injured innocence. "And we were all needed. The other Doctors all co-operated to some extent, but I – I objected." [...]
>
> "That's what I call being brave," muttered Ace.'[136]

In *Timewyrm: Revelation*'s (sometimes overly explicit) symbolic scheme, the fifth Doctor is said to be 'the Doctor's conscience'[137],

---

[135] Cornell, Paul, *Love and War* pp215, 217, 230-31.
[136] Cornell, Paul, *Timewyrm: Revelation*, p193.
[137] *Timewyrm: Revelation*, p191.

tormented by the acts he must perform to defeat his enemies. The words 'conscience' and 'objected' coming in such close succession must recall the term 'conscientious objector', applied to a principled non-combatant in time of war (and abbreviated to 'conchie', which is how Tim describes himself during the War coda of *Human Nature* [NA])[138]. Intriguingly, given the shift in emphasis between *Human Nature* [NA] and *Human Nature / The Family of Blood* (especially as regards Tim's role in the War), the fifth Doctor's heroism lies precisely in his refusal to contribute to his successor's war effort.

Gods, Lonely and Otherwise

There is another sense, though, in which this passage is crucial to interpreting *Human Nature / The Family of Blood*. In the notes to the 2002 online edition, Cornell expressed his surprise in hindsight that *Human Nature* [NA]:

> '...contains quite a few touchstones to my current religious point of view, which I try not to call anything, but which boils down to a passionate correspondence between Anglicanism and Paganism.'[139]

Cornell is here describing his worldview as it stood seven years after the first publication of *Human Nature* [NA], and more than a decade after that of *Timewyrm: Revelation*. Nonetheless, it is apparent throughout his novels for Virgin that both Christian and pagan myth-systems held a strong emotional resonance for him during the early 1990s. Like *Father's Day, Timewyrm: Revelation* is

---

[138] *Human Nature* [NA] p267.

[139] Cornell, notes on Chapter 4, *Human Nature* [NA], ebook, 348.

set largely in a (sentient) church, and a vicar is a major character. *Love and War*'s Jan is part of a Neopagan Traveller community whose rituals are described in detail. *Happy Endings* brings back both sets of characters, and takes Benny and her fiancé Jason through both an Anglican wedding and a pagan handfasting. Despite his professed surprise, it would have been more unexpected if Cornell had not included similar themes in *Human Nature* [NA].

In this context, the hanging of the Doctor's fifth self from an archetypal 'world tree'[140] can be read as a recapitulation both of the Norse god Odin's suffering of a similar ordeal on the World Tree Yggdrasil to gain the wisdom of the runes[141], and of the crucifixion of Jesus in the Gospels in atonement for humanity's sins[142]. As with both these divine figures, 'A wound had been inflicted' on the fifth Doctor, 'a great incision in his side'[143].

In the Old Norse devotional poem *Hávamál*, Odin's ritual suffering is described as a consecration of Odin to himself[144], and in the

---

[140] *Timewyrm: Revelation*, p188.

[141] *Hávamál: The Lay of the High One* 138 (Orchard, Andy, ed and trans, *The Elder Edda* p35). A runic inscription – which Ace recognises as the Doctor's signature – does feature in the sequence in *Timewyrm: Revelation* (p190), but the wisdom the Doctor gains takes the form of a flower, a symbol of enlightenment first used in *The Time Monster*.

[142] 'Who his own self bare our sins in his own body on the tree' (*I Peter* 2:24). The association of the cross with a tree, often contrasted with the equally significant tree in the Garden of Eden in *Genesis*, has a long history in Christian symbolism.

[143] *Timewyrm: Revelation*, p190; *Hávamál* 138; *John* 19:34.

[144] See Orchard, *The Elder Edda* p276.

Christian tradition too, God is both the victim and the recipient of the sacrifice[145]. Accordingly, while it is the seventh Doctor who ordains the suffering of his anthropomorphised conscience, he is also its victim, as the fifth Doctor is an aspect of himself. (As of 1991, the fifth Doctor was the only incarnation who had consciously sacrificed himself to save the life of another person, his companion Peri, and so was particularly well-suited to fulfil such a role[146].)

The implication of such an act of self-sacrifice is, of course, to cast the Doctor himself as a god. Cornell's approach to this idea as a writer of (albeit unconventional) faith is inevitably different from the largely secular sensibility the TV series has traditionally brought to it.

The motif has an inauspicious history in televised **Doctor Who** prior to 2007. The Doctor's impersonation of Zeus in *The Myth Makers* (1965) backfires when the deception is discovered; worse still, his Trojan companion Katarina's continuing belief in his divine nature is arguably a contributing factor in her untimely death[147]. In *The Face of Evil* (1977), where a supercomputer inadvertently imprinted with his identity has set itself up as a deity, both the Tesh who believe the Doctor is their god and Leela's people for whom he is the Evil

---

[145] 'He sacrificed for our sins. Where did he find the sacrifice? Where did he find the victim which he would offer pure? Other he found none; his own self he offered.' (St Augustine, *Homilies on the First Epistle of John*, 7:9.)

[146] *The Caves of Androzani* (1984). Cornell's co-written fifth Doctor audio story 'Winter' (Cornell, Paul, and Mike Maddox, *Circular Time* (2007)) is another psychodrama, this time taking place in the Doctor's mind at the moment of this sacrifice.

[147] In 'The Traitors' (*The Daleks' Master Plan* episode 4, 1965).

One must be disabused of their superstitious errors. Prompted by Margaret the Slitheen's awe at the TARDIS in *Boom Town*, he tells her, 'Don't worship me, I'd make a very bad god.'

Russell T Davies appears to agree. *Human Nature / The Family of Blood* falls within a loose long-term story arc about the Doctor's status in the universe. After redeeming Rose through the somewhat messianic death of his ninth self in *The Parting of the Ways*, there are several low-key references to the 10th Doctor as a divine figure, beginning with the prophecy in *New Earth* (2006) that the Face of Boe will deliver his last words to 'a wanderer [...] the man without a home. The lonely god' – a figure who, in *Gridlock* (2007) is confirmed to be the Doctor himself. In *Utopia* (2007), the Doctor will let slip what might have qualified him for this status:

> 'She came back. Opened the heart of the TARDIS and absorbed the Time Vortex itself. [...] No one's ever meant to have that power. If a Time Lord did that, he'd become a god. A vengeful god. But she was human.'

While the ninth Doctor was not the one who opened the heart of the TARDIS, it was absorbing the Time Vortex from Rose that triggered his regeneration.

In the season finale, *Last of the Time Lords* (2007), it is humanity's expression of its faith in the Doctor (as promulgated by Martha during her pilgrimage across the devastated Earth), and referred to explicitly by the Master as a 'prayer', which restores the Doctor from a decrepit state and enables him to forgive, rather than taking revenge on, the Master. The theme develops beyond 2007[148], reaching its peak in *The Waters of Mars* (2009) where the Doctor assumes the power of life and death over the whole crew of Bowie Base. In an essay for *Time and Relative Dimensions in Faith* (2013), Michael Charlton describes this as a 'moment of spiritual crisis' in which the Doctor 'begins to claim godhood for himself.'[149] After Steven Moffat's arrival as showrunner in 2010, the focus moves from the Doctor's claim to godhood to the more humbling question of whether he is 'a good man', but his tendency to arrogate divine prerogatives is revisited in, among other stories, Toby Whithouse's *The God Complex* (2011)[150] and Moffat's own *Hell Bent* (2015).

Human Nature / The Family of Blood does not make overt reference to this continuing plotline, but it is not reticent in describing the Doctor in terms which recall divinity:

---

[148] In, for instance, the Doctor and Donna's adoption as Roman household deities in *The Fires of Pompeii*,

[149] Charlton, Michael, 'The Doctor Working on God's Time: Kairos and Intervention in *The Waters of Mars* and *A Christmas Carol*', pp69, 71. Crome, Andrew and James McGrath, eds, *Time and Relative Dimensions in Faith: Religion and Doctor Who*.

[150] See Driscoll, Paul, *The Black Archive #9: The God Complex* (2017), for a detailed examination of this story's place in the Doctor's character arc.

'I've seen him. He's like fire and ice and rage. He's like the night and the storm in the heart of the sun. [...] He's ancient and forever. He burns at the centre of time and he can see the turn of the universe. [...] And he's wonderful.'

[Tim, *The Family of Blood*][151]

Justice and Vengeance

As Timothy's description echoes divine terminology, the awe with which 'Baines's final narration is delivered displays similar elements. A question hangs over the resolution of *Human Nature / The Family of Blood*. The Doctor, characterised as 'never cruel or cowardly', metes out to the Family a terrible punishment that could very well be considered cruel. 'Baines' describes how the Doctor's retreat into Smith's persona was an act of mercy, in allowing the Family to live out their natural lifespan without finding him, but there seems to be very little mercy in his eventual treatment of them[152]. How can we explain this?

On a personal level for the character, we might consider the possibility that this is the Doctor unleashed, that through his anger at being forced to give up his human identity he is expressing the cruelty that under normal circumstances he overcomes. As we have seen, the Doctor can be cowardly, therefore the constant reinforcement of 'never cruel or cowardly' as his personal ethos suggests that perhaps the temptation to be both is ever present,

[151] Cornell notes that this description was written by Davies ('Introduction' to *Human Nature* [NA], 2015 ed, ppvi-vii).
[152] *The Family of Blood*.

and it is an act of active will that supresses this[153]. This makes it more of a powerful idealistic personal objective than a descriptor; the Doctor is the Doctor because he makes the effort to be his best self, as opposed to the possible alternatives[154].

The fact that this is one of the few times that we do see the Doctor acting unfettered to hand out what seems more like vengeance and retribution than justice is a reflection of just how strongly his emotions have been affected by his experiences as Smith, and the depth of his anger at having been made to give it up. He asks Joan to go with him, and she refuses, admonishing him at the same time. It is not often that the Doctor is entirely thwarted by the consequences of his own choices rather than unkind fate. As we discussed in Chapter 2, this 10th Doctor does appear to have some cold and selfish tendencies, and the outburst of anger from beneath a veneer of charm and pleasantry may be another symptom of his disordered emotional state as a result of his traumatic War experiences.

However, some answers may be also found by continuing the examination of the Doctor as an analogue of a divine being. Vengeance is a divine quality as much as mercy, particularly (in the Abrahamic tradition) in the Old Testament. While the mercy of God is still an important characteristic, it may be tempered with vengeance when the latter is justified by disobedience. Certainly

---

[153] This is a theme to which Moffat's episodes have returned a number of times, notably in *A Good Man Goes to War* and *The Witch's Familiar* (2015).

[154] Perhaps the Valeyard, the evil future (or potential) Doctor played by Michael Jayston in *The Trial of a Time Lord* (1986), results from a possible alternative path in which this goal is not achieved.

'the fury of the Time Lord' has the qualities of divine punishment: in their various ways all four of the Family of Blood are imprisoned forever, a fate which entails yet also mocks the eternal life which they had been so ruthlessly seeking. The irony of this recalls the customised punishments given to various offenders in the classical Tartarus and such descriptions of the Christian Hell as Dante's *Inferno*, which were also supposed to last eternally. 'Baines's comment that 'This Doctor, who'd fought with gods and demons [...] was being kind,' places the Doctor on an equal footing with the divine while alluding to the paradox that the Christian God, who punishes sinners permanently in Hell, is described as merciful.

In this light, and given the quote that concludes the previous section, it is not unnatural that Smith finds Tim's characterisation of his alter ego terrifying – and indeed, Tim admits that he 'was so scared' of the Doctor he discovered inside the watch[155].

Resurrection and Regeneration

In *Human Nature* [NA], Timothy Dean has a rather different relationship with the Doctor inside the Pod, taking on many of his qualities until it is implied that he is on the verge of becoming him[156]. One such effect is that he becomes blasé about his own death. Here are his thoughts at a moment of brutal bullying at the hands of a clique led by Hutchinson: 'Let them, the voice inside him said. Hang me, cut me down, spread my blood on the field. End my

---

[155] *The Family of Blood*.

[156] See for instance *Human Nature* [NA] p203:

> 'Tim paused, looking at the Pod. "If I put it to my head, I'd change, wouldn't I?"
> "You'd become the Doctor, I suppose. Do you want to?"'

life. I'll return.'[157] And indeed, Tim is apparently killed by being hanged from a window, his 'cold body' concealed by his peers. When he emerges from this state, he and others see it as a resurrection: '"I died [...] And then I came back."'[158]

Rather than a 'regeneration', as **Doctor Who** uses the term, this miracle is ascribed to Tim acquiring the 'respiratory bypass system' characteristic of Gallifreyan physiology[159]. The book has already stated that 'Time Lord biodata had that effect on living things, making them more like Time Lords,' and notably the resurrected Tim is also said to have two hearts[160]. In any case, Tim's apparent return from the dead is typical of the Doctor's own periodic deaths and resurrections. Cornell notes that 'Tim's thoughts on going out of the window are exactly where this stuff' – his 'passionate correspondence between Anglicanism and Paganism' – 'connects to **Who** for me'[161]. Though couched in language reminiscent of the seventh Doctor's TV persona[162], the process described in Tim's inner monologue is evidently that of a symbolic sacrifice – recalling the pagan idea of a crop god whose yearly death and rebirth mirror, and ritually induce, the cycle of seasonal regrowth of the

---

[157] *Human Nature* [NA] p84.
[158] *Human Nature* [NA] pp100-01.
[159] First mentioned in *Pyramids of Mars*. A dream sequence further ties Tim's near-death experience to the **New Adventures** mythology of Time, Pain, Death and Life, the Eternals who act as Gods of Gallifrey.
[160] *Human Nature* [NA] pp63, 123. In the Virgin books' continuity, the first Doctor has only one heart, acquiring the second during his first regeneration.
[161] Cornell, notes on Chapter 4, *Human Nature* [NA], ebook, p348.
[162] The defiant 'End my life' in particular quotes both *The Happiness Patrol* episode 2 (1988) and *Battlefield* (1989) episode 4.

vegetation he embodies[163]. As Cornell implies, Anglican Christianity, certain strands of Neopaganism, and – thanks to the mechanism of regeneration – **Doctor Who** all have at their heart figures of awe who die and are resurrected.

Something of the pagan element of this dynamic survives in the television story. As men made of vegetation, the scarecrows introduced by Davies somewhat resemble pagan crop gods. They also recollect the modern 'folk horror' genre inspired by European rural folklore and folk ritual[164]. The transformation of the temporally-frozen 'Baines' into one of their number is more suggestive, as it involves placing him on a cross-shaped wooden frame and setting him 'to work, standing over the fields of England, as their protector.'[165] Again, a man who is not a man is affixed to a piece of a tree; again this is said to be for the benefit of the fields; but this time the sacrificial subject is not the same person as the god at whose behest this is done – he is more literally a victim, though hardly a blameless one[166].

---

[163] This general analysis of a recurring mythological theme originates with Sir JG Frazer's *The Golden Bough* (1890). Like much pioneering 19th-century scholarship, it continues to be influential in popular culture – including, in this case, reconstructionist religion – despite having been largely superseded in academia.

[164] Animate scarecrows have a prior association with **Doctor Who**, in Jon Pertwee's title role in **Worzel Gummidge** (1978-81), which at least one commentator has linked with the folk horror genre (Williams, Owen, 'A History of British Folk Horror'). For further background, see Scovell, Adam, 'Where to Begin with Folk Horror'.

[165] *The Family of Blood*.

[166] Cornell's 2017 novel *Chalk* again returns to the idea of pagan sacrifice, among many other concerns which characterise *Human Nature / The Family of Blood*, the rest of Cornell's **Doctor Who**

As we shall see in Chapter 5, this motif of sacrifice – echoed in more myth-systems than just those of Norse paganism and Christianity – is one element of a wider archetypal scheme. For the moment, though, suffice it to say that *Human Nature / The Family of Blood* is more recognisably Christian than pagan in its symbolism.

As with *Father's Day*, with its church setting and its monsters that loosely resemble the devils of Christianity, much of this association is achieved cosmetically. Leaving aside the pre-credits sequence of *Human Nature* [TV], the story opens with the singing of a hymn, John Bunyan's 'To Be A Pilgrim', and ends with a Remembrance Day ceremony conducted by a Church of England priest. While the Bunyan hymn effects some foreshadowing for the season's later episodes – dropping the names of the Master and the *Valiant*[167], and hinting at Martha's globetrotting pilgrimage[168] – it also

---

work and his oeuvre in general: bullying, morally ambiguous doppelgangers, doomed love, relationship with the landscape and the school as a microcosm of society.

[167] 'To Be a Pilgrim' exists in variant versions; the one sung in *Human Nature / The Family of Blood* is No 402 in Dearmer, Percy, and Ralph Vaughan Williams, eds, *The English Hymnal* (1906). Bunyan's original does not mention 'the Master', and refers to 'valour' rather than using the word 'valiant' (Bunyan, John, *The Pilgrim's Progress* pp297-98).

[168] These become relevant in *Utopia, The Sound of Drums* and *Last of the Time Lords* respectively. Cornell notes that he did not select the hymn, and speculates that it might have been Davies' idea; the director, Charles Palmer, suggests that this emerged from production discussion (*Human Nature* [TV] DVD commentary). We might presume that the specific choice of hymn was based on its mention of 'the Master', and that this in turn influenced the naming of the *Valiant*.

reinforces that the school is an Anglican foundation, whose pupils and teachers are expected to participate in Christian worship. (Earlier in the season, *Gridlock* deployed 'The Old Rugged Cross' and 'Abide with Me' to a similar purpose, illustrating the shared community values of the motorists of New New York.) The second verse, with its combative imagery ('No foes shall stay his might / Though he with giants fight'), recurs during the battle scene with the scarecrows in *The Family of Blood*, emphasising the cultural link between the school's Christian ethos and the military virtues Rocastle and Smith have tried to instil in the boys[169].

By contrast the text with which the story finishes, an excerpt from Lawrence Binyon's 'For the Fallen', is elegiac rather than martial, but is still among the most conventional of war poems, sentimentalising and glorifying the First World War's dead while doing nothing to question its pretexts. The fact that the poem is being read by a vicar again lends this viewpoint the weight of Christian orthodoxy. The vicar's gender may be intended to denote the progress the Church of England has made during the intervening 94 years[170], but the assumptions underlying the small

---

[169] Murray Gold observes on the *Human Nature* [TV] DVD commentary that 'To Be a Pilgrim' is 'a martial hymn'.

[170] Assuming that the story's coda takes place in the present day, i.e. 2007, and thus that Tim is one of the last surviving First World War combat veterans. If we further assume that Tim in 1913 is 17, the same age as Thomas Sangster in 2007, this would make the 21st-century Tim 111 years old. Given that the earliest ordinations of women in the Church of England took place in 1994, and Tim is clearly old enough to fight in 1914-18, his mid-90s are the youngest he can possible be here. Huw Rees, who plays the elderly Tim, was 83 in 2007 (personal correspondence with author).

portion of the ceremony we see are wholly compatible with Rocastle's rhetoric of 'a just and proper war'[171].

That said, there is no explicit discussion of Christianity in the televised story. The novel, without emphasising it especially strongly, nonetheless uses it for more than historical set dressing: for instance, when Constance jokes that 'God saved' the King from her attempt to upset his pony and trap during a suffragette protest; when Rocastle suggests that enemy soldiers 'whose creed is unchristian' should not be extended the consideration of civilised combat; when Hadleman explains that his own faith is not in God but in 'dialectical materialism'; and even when Smith – who remembers having 'grown up without religion' – attempts a clumsy prayer in the village church[172]. The television story, presumably wary of alienating a popular audience unfamiliar with, and likely uninterested in, the conventions of Christianity, couches its political and moral discussions in secular terms – though there are two passing references to 'God's earth'[173], which interestingly again connects the concept of divinity with that of the land.

At a more fundamental level, however, the premise of the story – in its literary and televised forms – is drawn from Christianity. While there are many legends of gods, including Odin, disguising themselves as men and women, the fundamental myth of Christianity is that God became completely human as Jesus of Nazareth. In *Human Nature / The Family of Blood*, the Doctor's

---

[171] *Human Nature* [TV].

[172] *Human Nature* [NA] pp187, 139, 215, 111.

[173] Once by Tim (quoting his uncle) in *Human Nature* [TV], once by Rocastle in *The Family of Blood*.

Smith persona originates as a disguise, but its effect is to make the Doctor a fully human being.

Different forms of Christianity apply varying interpretations to this central doctrine. Some hold that the incarnation was necessary so that Jesus could validly be punished in humanity's place for human sin, while others stress an empathic God's own need to share the suffering of his creation. The humanity of John Smith fulfils neither of these purposes. It is true that Smith, to quote the biblical Timothy, 'came into the world to save sinners'[174] – specifically the Family – from the wrath of the divine being whose incarnation he represents. Nevertheless, his death is necessary, not to atone for anyone's sins (except possibly the Doctor's own, in bringing the Family to Earth), but because once they have arrived only a Time Lord is adequate for the task of defeating them. And, while the novel's Doctor is partly motivated by wanting to share Benny's pain at the loss of love, for the TV Doctor this outcome is purely accidental.

In fact, aside from being regarded as a teacher and having a friend called Martha[175], Smith is not an especially close analogue for Jesus. Where the latter was a member of a subjugated people living on the margins of an oppressive empire, Smith belongs to a nation

---

[174] *I Timothy* 1:16. It is doubtful that this is the significance of Tim's name.

[175] Interestingly, given Martha's unwilling role as a maid in *Human Nature / The Family of Blood*, the biblical Martha is best known for her annoyance that her sister Mary of Bethany is paying too much attention to Jesus rather than helping her with their domestic tasks (*Luke* 10:40). A comparison with Joan would probably be uncharitable.

of imperialists whose overseas exploits he does nothing to question[176]. Though his feat in saving a baby with a throw of a cricket-ball appears miraculous, demonstrations of athletic precision are hardly the style of miracle associated with Jesus. A case might be made that the creation of Smith's persona by the TARDIS (consistently personified, when it is at all, as female) counts as a form of 'virgin birth', but it would be a very tenuous one. Most obviously, while the Gospels ascribe to Jesus no interest in romance[177], it is Smith's love for Joan that comes to define his humanity, and which creates the strongest conflict with the universe's need for him to sacrifice himself.

The Last Temptation of Mr Chips

Paradoxically, though, it is here that the single clearest correspondence between Smith and Jesus emerges – though not with the Jesus of the Gospels, but rather with the character played by Willem Dafoe in Martin Scorsese's film *The Last Temptation of Christ* (1988).

Following the 1955 novel of the same name by Nikos Kazantzakis, Scorsese depicts Jesus as a conflicted figure, his human and divine natures perennially at odds. In the film, the temptations traditionally faced by Jesus in the desert unfold with modifications,

---

[176] Notably David Tennant continues to use an English accent, rather than reverting to his natural Scottish one – another point of departure from the novel, whose seventh Doctor retains Sylvester McCoy's Scottish accent as Dr Smith (*Human Nature* [NA] p65).

[177] For simplicity's sake we will assume that the Gospels can be read together as a consensus account of Jesus' life, since highlighting their divergences is well beyond the scope of a 180-page book on an old **Doctor Who** story.

as do various other biblical incidents. But the cinema version ends with a much more startling departure from the Gospel narrative. During the crucifixion itself, as Jesus is dying in agony, an angel appears to him (much as Ace does to the fifth Doctor in *Timewyrm: Revelation*) and gives him the option of rescue, which he accepts. Leaving with the angel, Scorsese's Jesus goes on to live a long and fulfilled life, marrying Mary Magdalen (and later, after her death, cohabiting with Mary of Bethany and her sister Martha) and fathering children. Eventually we see him on his deathbed during the siege of Jerusalem in 70 CE, being accused by the elderly Judas, who has also survived, of betraying his disciples by failing to go through with his appointed death. Realising that his apparent guardian angel is in fact Satan, the aged Jesus drags himself painfully to Golgotha, the site of the crucifixion, where he prays to resume his punishment. As if no time has passed, the crucifixion scene is restored and God's plan proceeds according to schedule.

The parallels with the premonition granted to Smith and Joan, of the future that would follow if Smith rejected the vocation to become the Doctor and remained himself, are partial but still striking[178]. In the parallel passage in *Human Nature* [NA], the vision

---

[178] This has been confirmed by Paul Cornell: 'It's very *Last Temptation*, I should have mentioned that' (comment #2072 on Cornell, 'The Family of Blood'). It has also been noted by numerous commentators: see, for instance, Burk, Graeme and Robert Smith?, *Who Is the Doctor: The Unofficial Guide to Doctor Who – The New Series* p156; Comer, Todd, 'Who Needs Family? I've Got the Whole World on My Shoulders: How the Doctor's Non-Domesticity Interrupts History' in Hansen, Christopher J, ed, *Rumours, Peregrinations and Regenerations: A Critical Approach to Doctor Who*, p38.

the Pod grants Smith and Tim is a warning, not a temptation: unless the Doctor returns, the Aubertides will conquer Gallifrey and kill his friends there[179]. In the Davies era there is no Gallifrey for the Family to conquer, but still, a victory for the family would result in 'destruction [...] war across the stars for every child'[180]. In making this merely a verbal warning, however, while the happy future Smith is sacrificing is seen directly, the adaptation makes his dilemma seem far more palpable.

In both *The Family of Blood* and *The Last Temptation of Christ*, the visions occur as the protagonist is contemplating his imminent demise, and offer him an alternative. Both tempt him with the promise that he may live a mundane life of ordinary experience, rather than being called upon to perform an act of exceptional self-sacrifice. Both promise marriage and children, which in the standard understanding of these protagonists' lives appear to be out of the question[181]. Both end with the protagonist in the process of dying of old age.

---

[179] *Human Nature* [NA] pp217-20. A surprising number of other characters also receive information about the future, which is then averted: Tim, about Rocastle's death; Torrence, about his own survival; and of course Alexander, about Richard's death at the Somme (*Human Nature* [NA] pp141, 144, 115).

[180] *The Family of Blood*.

[181] The question is, in fact, more complicated than this. The Gospels are silent on the question of Jesus's sexuality and marital status, rather than imposing the celibacy often ascribed to him; while the Doctor has always been a grandfather ('An Unearthly Child'), and will in a year or so meet his future wife (*Silence in the Library / Forest of the Dead*).

Both also appear in some sense to be no mere vision, but actual alternative histories. Jesus's revelation anticipates historical events including the fall of Jerusalem and the rise of Christianity (as disseminated by Paul of Tarsus), and Judas' behaviour is what might be expected of the character in this historical reality, rather than in a fiction generated by Satan. And, unless we ascribe some sinister motive to the Doctor's pocket-watch, it must be assumed that it is granting Smith a literal vision of a genuine, if mutable, future; the appearance of convincing 1920s fashions acts as corroborating evidence for this[182]. If they are indeed real, both of these timelines are averted as the protagonists surrender to their respective fates and their worlds are saved.

(Interestingly, this reverses the central conceit of *Imzadi*, the **Star Trek: The Next Generation** novel that Cornell cited as an influence on *Human Nature* [NA]. There, as in *The Last Temptation of Christ*, the future which turns out to be 'incorrect' is assumed to be real until the elderly hero returns to his past to set it right. In *Imzadi*'s case, however, Deanna must survive, rather than die, in order to set history back on its correct path.)

As noted, there are also obvious differences, primarily that Smith's temptation takes up less than a minute of screen time and leads into the climax of the plot and a lengthy coda, whereas that of Jesus lasts for some 26 minutes and is followed only by a brief return to the crucifixion scene. Smith and Joan seem well aware that they are being shown a vision, whereas Jesus believes that he is living his actual life until he makes a decision within that future to

---

[182] Cornell refers to it as 'the flash forwards to the couple's future together' ('Adapting the Novel for the Screen' p361).

reject it. We see little enough of Smith's future to believe that it is an uncomplicatedly happy one (notably, there is no hint that he and Joan might be affected by the imminent War), whereas Jesus's is a realistic mixture of joy and pain.

Nonetheless, the similarities are sufficient to suggest that *The Last Temptation of Christ* is not merely a strong influence on *Human Nature / The Family of Blood*, but the most direct evidence of Christian influence in it[183]. For the viewer it certainly acts to focus, reify and render more moving the tragic decision that Smith must make.

The Empty Man

Unlike the conventional image of Jesus (but in common with Cornell's other sacrificial victim, Pete Tyler), John Smith himself is no paragon of human virtue. Though morally no worse than the average human being, he is shown by turns to be patronising, pompous, cowardly, indecisive, selfish and unthinkingly tolerant of cruelty. We see him make idiotic racist assumptions, panic in response to pressure and aim (though not fire) a gun.

Ultimately, of course, Smith proves altruistic, selfless and astonishingly brave, but the traditional Christian conception of Jesus would allow for none of these vices he has also displayed (though Scorsese's might concede the possibility of some). In a

[183] An odd further parallel is that both visual works are adaptations of novels that themselves reinterpret from a radical perspective an existing 'canon', many of whose devotees are capable of generating disproportionate controversy when it is suggested that their central character might under some circumstances participate in sex. But it is perhaps possible to stretch the analogy too far.

sense, this means that the Doctor as Smith is more human than God as Jesus, because he is allowed to be flawed.

Writing in *Time and Relative Dimensions in Faith* about *Human Nature* [NA] and *Human Nature / The Family of Blood*, K Jason Wardley talks about 'kenosis' or 'self-emptying': the doctrine that Jesus 'either withheld or voluntarily relinquished certain divine prerogatives during his incarnation'[184]. This is generally used to support an enjoinder to Christlike humility, and Wardley goes on to speak about the value of ethical kenosis to break cycles of violence in the story (though this is clearer in the pacifism of the novel than on screen). The rhetoric of 'self-emptying', however, recalls the Doctor's assertion to Joan that 'everything that John Smith is and was, I'm capable of that, too'[185]: a statement which contrasts, as we have seen, with the novel Doctor's claim that Smith is 'a character I created, a fiction' – albeit one who is 'the same shape of person'. Where the seventh Doctor alleges that 'There is no human part' of him[186], the 10th Doctor's persona is said to encompass everything that Smith's does.

This, at least, is the Doctor's own assessment. An earlier exchange between Smith and Joan comes to a different conclusion:

SMITH

Did you see?

---

[184] Wardley, K Jason, 'Divine and Human Nature: Incarnation and Kenosis in **Doctor Who**', p33. Crome and McGrath, eds, *Time and Relative Dimensions in Faith*.

[185] *The Family of Blood*.

[186] *Human Nature* [NA] p256.

JOAN

The Time Lord has such adventures, but he could never have a life like that.

SMITH

And yet I could.

Accordingly, Joan (who has earlier told Smith that 'If he's not you, I don't want him to [love me]') rejects his offer to take her with him in the TARDIS, telling him 'John Smith is dead, and you look like him.'[187]

However, this is consistent with the idea of kenosis, in that it is only via the process of stripping himself of certain attributes that the alien, eternal Time Lord may become capable of participation in mundane human events and states like love and family. Whether or not the Doctor is truly able to love Joan in his own right, his metamorphosis into a being able to have a human, grounded experience of the world gives him a perspective which his fully Time Lord self could never have gained. His reaction to meeting Joan's great-granddaughter in *The End of Time* episode 2 suggests that this growth in understanding has accompanied him throughout his 10th incarnation; that, in fact, it may have changed him[188].

---

[187] *The Family of Blood*. The seventh Doctor's assertion that Smith's emotions are ones he cannot share are also undermined, by the tears that only Wolsey the cat witnesses (*Human Nature* [NA] p260).

[188] The idea that God would be lesser without the incarnation – that God needed the experience of humanity in order to become complete – would be anathema in conventional Christianity, where

Whether the Doctor's self-diagnosis can be trusted or not, his assertions lead us to believe that – while *Human Nature* [NA]'s Dr John Smith is similar to, but distinct from, the seventh Doctor – *Human Nature / The Family of Blood*'s Mr John Smith is a **subset** of the 10th Doctor. He is a Doctor, in other words, from whom certain aspects – certain Time Lord prerogatives – have been emptied out.

We might assume that these consisted largely of the Doctor's superhuman mental and physical abilities (just as humanised Superman of the 1980 film *Superman II* – another source often cited by Cornell[189] – cannot fly, is no longer invulnerable, lacks superhuman strength and so forth); and certainly Joan's medical examination attests that Smith has only a single heart. But the incident with the cricket-ball and the pram suggests that at least some of these remain, accessible to Smith at moments of abstraction.

Indeed, the most important thing Smith seems to be lacking is the Doctor's cosmic perspective – the big-picture thinking, and the ability to draw moral conclusions from it, which would enable him to see at once that training children 'to defend the king and all his citizens and properties'[190] is servile and jingoistic, and that giving

---

the incarnation takes place for humanity's benefit rather than God's. However, it is compatible with the (arguably post-) Christian offshoot of 'process theology', where God is in a long-term collaboration with creation in a process of becoming fully divine, and where Jesus is only the most perfect instance of an incarnation which embraces all of humanity ('Process Theology' in Hinnells, John R, *The Penguin Dictionary of Religions*, p258).

[189] For instance in in *Alter Ego*, the episode of **Doctor Who Confidential** broadcast alongside *Human Nature* [TV].

[190] *The Family of Blood*.

the older ones permission to beat the younger is abhorrent[191]. Imprisoned as he is within the perspective of a middle-class Edwardian schoolteacher, Smith needs considerably longer, and the help of Joan, to reach this insight – although she couches this in terms of his coming to understand himself better ('John Smith wouldn't want them to fight, never mind the Doctor'[192]).

The Doctor's perspective may well be a prerogative of a Time Lord, or even of a god, but emptying himself of it has not made the TV's Smith more Christlike. Indeed, it has resulted not in a breaking of cycles of violence but, initially at least, a willingness to perpetuate them. Part of the babbling that Tim hears emerging from the pocket-watch – in the Doctor's own voice – is 'Keep me away from the false and empty man,' recalling the 'Hollow Men' of Eliot's poem [193]. This may refer to 'Baines' – who certainly qualifies – but it could also mean Smith, suggesting that some part of the Doctor's psyche sees the latter not merely as a reduced version of himself but as a deceptive shell. Interestingly though, the arrogance and vanity which might be diagnosed as the 10th Doctor's own besetting sins are largely absent from Smith, replaced with an insecurity and shyness which make him a likeable character despite his moral myopia. (This reflects the dichotomy between conventional perceptions of the all-powerful God the Father and the meek and humble Jesus.)

Smith's incarnate existence is also a distinctly partial one. While he is said to be fully human, and (based on the flashforward sequence)

---

[191] *Human Nature* [TV].
[192] *The Family of Blood*.
[193] *Human Nature* [TV].

seemingly has the standard life expectancy of someone of his time, background and apparent physical age, it seems he is in fact alive for less than three months[194]. He was never born, and misses out on the mundane human experiences of infancy, childhood and adolescence, as well as the more conditional ones of marriage, parenthood and old age[195]. Though they fall in love, he and Joan have no opportunity for sex, which many would consider another defining (if again not universal) feature of biological humanity. Smith does not even experience death as such, though the cessation of existence which the pocket-watch heralds is as terrifying to him, and may even (judging by the Doctor's original transformation) be equivalently painful[196]. In comparison with the Gospels' Jesus, who lives a complete human life up to the point of his death and who dies, if not normally, at least in a manner not uncommon for a dissident subject of the Roman empire, Smith's incarnation is evanescent and superficial.

Most of all, given the TV story's focus (a stronger one than in the novel), it seems clear that a full participation by Smith in the humanity of his age would involve him serving in the forthcoming

---

[194] This is the stated lifetime of the Family (*The Family of Blood*). (It is also the length of time the novel's Doctor expects his human avatar to last (*Human Nature* [NA] p9).) Smith has known Joan for 'two months' in *Human Nature* [TV], roughly the length of time from the start of a standard school year to 10 November.

[195] By contrast, the Master appears to have become incarnate as a child and lived to old age (*Utopia*), though his aims were different in detail and he presumably had no short-lived human companion to consider.

[196] The novel's Smith has a more complex – and in the end, thanks to the **New Adventures**' 'Gods of Gallifrey' mythos, a literal – encounter with Death (*Human Nature* [NA] p247).

First World War. Though he is certainly of combat age, and healthy, there is no hint in his vision of the future that this would ever have happened. (We might guess that, were he to remain Smith, Martha would somehow fulfil the Doctor's instruction to keep him from 'getting involved in big historical events'[197].)

Which returns us to Tim. In the novel, Timothy Dean's identification with the Doctor is a close one, and there is a strong hint that it has changed him for life. He experiences the War (though not as a combatant), saves Richard Hadleman's life and goes on to live until 1995, by which time he has a great-grandchild[198]. His is, clearly, a fully human and humane life, and it is one the Doctor has given him, through his resurrection following his early death at school[199].

Certainly the identification is less clear-cut in the TV story, but there, too, Tim seemingly goes on to live the kind of life Smith has been deprived of, a fulfilling one that partakes fully in the human experience. We see him save Hutchinson, who tormented him at school, from his destined death in the War – a Doctorish act of forgiveness and altruism facilitated by his own foreknowledge and by the (now ordinarily functional) watch that the Doctor bequeaths him. Though this aspect of the novel is diluted on TV – and in the novel it lacks the contrast with Smith's flashforward temptation – it may be that, in some platonic and ideal version of *Human Nature* in which the best aspects of the novel and the TV episodes were

---

[197] *Human Nature* [TV].

[198] *Human Nature* [NA] pp267-69.

[199] Though it might be argued that, without the cavalier attitude to death granted him by the Pod, he would have struggled more actively for life, and thus perhaps not died in the first place.

combined, it would be Tim who became the truly incarnational figure.

CHAPTER 5: HERO AND SUPERHERO

In his introduction to the reprint of *Human Nature* [NA], Cornell says that the idea for the novel came from a wish 'to dig deep again, write something meaningful' after his third **New Adventure**, *No Future* (1994), was given negative reviews. As he recounts the thought process:

> 'What I really wanted to do was give the Doctor a full-blown romance, but I couldn't think of a way to do that that would be acceptable to my editors and to the audience.'

He mentions Peter David's *Imzadi*, which he says 'did exactly what I wanted to do: broke the perceived rules of the franchise'. He continues:

> 'It suddenly occurred to me that there was an archetypal story shape that did everything I was after, and which **Doctor Who** had never used. Or as the thought was framed in my head: "*Superman II* works every time."'[200]

---

[200] Cornell, 'Introduction' to Human Nature [NA] pv. This does not necessarily contradict the claim that he wrote the earliest version of the story while at school – *Human Nature* [NA] is a complex narrative, and may well have had an equally complex genesis involving multiple moments of inspiration. One might suppose that the young Cornell wrote fanfiction where the Doctor becomes human as a response to watching *Superman II* (released in the UK

The Superhero's Journey

The film *Superman II*, like *Human Nature* [NA] and *Human Nature / The Family of Blood*, is the story of an alien with two personas, mortal and immortal, who must choose between the mutually exclusive options of life as a human with his beloved, and a celibate existence wielding his divine powers to save the world. However, this synopsis largely exhausts the similarities, and many aspects of the film are at odds with their equivalents in Cornell's novel and scripts.

Most obviously, the device of its eponymous protagonist becoming human is a brief interlude in *Superman II*'s romantic subplot, rather than its primary focus. This excursion, from the idea first being mooted to the last we see of the humanised Kal-El, lasts less than 15 minutes of the two-hour film (and does not even fill that screentime, much of which is taken up with the ascendancy in Superman's absence of his fellow Kryptonian, General Zod)[201].

Superman's human persona, Clark Kent, is not the humanised Superman as John Smith is the humanised Doctor, but rather a disguise the superhero consciously assumes to put humans at their ease. While Superman is posing as Clark, he retains his self-awareness and his superpowers; indeed, when he loses these powers he seems to abandon the pretence. In contrast with Smith's

---

when he was 13), and that the adult novelist later recalled the idea as a solution to the dilemma he outlines.

[201] This contrasts with the relationship we observed between *Human Nature / The Family of Blood* and *The Last Temptation of Christ*, where a primary element of the film inspires a brief passage in the TV story.

situation, Kent retains all of Superman's core personality along with all his memories.

Equally, while the love between Smith and Joan is an outcome of Smith's humanity, Superman elects to become human (or 'mortal' as his mother's recording puts it, making the mythic origins of the archetype rather too explicit) in response to his romance with Lois Lane. Though Superman ostensibly reacquires his superhumanity in order to defeat Zod, this follows a realisation on his part that a human Kal-El is no longer the man Lois fell in love with – she has always loved Superman, not Clark. Unlike Joan, Lois loves the god, not the man, though only the latter can have a relationship with her[202].

Finally, the film spares us the agony of choice which we see Smith and Joan suffer. Superman's decisions, first to renounce and then to reacquire his powers, are presented to us – and to Lois, who is permitted as little input into her lover's life choices as Martha's is into the Doctor's – as done deals. At the end of the film Superman (chivalrously or abusively, depending on whether one applies the prevalent sexual politics of 1980 or 2017) erases Lois's memories of his dual identity, imposing on her an unawareness of their time together which parallels Smith's ignorance about his own past as the Doctor. We see no sign that the restored Superman feels other than serenely untroubled by this, or by the humanity he has lost.

In detail, therefore, the parallels are few. Indeed, at a level below that of the high concept, the most obvious point of similarity

---

[202] At least, this is what we are told by the recording of Superman's mother. As she also insists that the loss of his powers will be permanent, the matter is perhaps open to question.

between *Superman II* and *Human Nature / The Family of Blood* is the scenic cliché (absent from the novel) of a baby in a pram imperilled by a falling object – and characteristically, while the child in *Human Nature* [TV] is saved by John Smith, it is the fully-superpowered Superman who rescues the infant in *Superman II*.

Prior to the paperback reprint, Cornell gave a fuller account of his thought processes in the 'Introduction' to the *Human Nature* ebook:

> '...nobody had ever really done mythologist Joseph Campbell's "Hero's Journey" for the Doctor, the plot that's most commonly recognised in popular culture as that of *Superman II*, where the hero gives everything up to discover what normal humanity is like. Fertile ground, I thought.'[203]

In a 2002 interview, he elaborates on '...the *Superman II* scenario where we learn who the character is by taking away his powers, associations, literary clothes, etc., to see what the essentials are.' He adds that David's *Imzadi* takes 'a similar burrowing-into stance with its characters'[204].

As a description of *Superman II* – and indeed of *Imzadi* – this feels like wishful thinking, but the reference to Joseph Campbell is illuminating[205]. Cornell had previously professed his admiration for the mythographer ('a guy who took all of the world's myths, folk tales, fairy tales and legends and distilled them to try and find a

---

[203] Cornell, *Human Nature* [ebook] p341.
[204] Ortiz, Julio Angel, 'Throwback Interview: Paul Cornell (2002)'.
[205] What follows will include a lot of references to 'Cornell' and 'Campbell', names which can look very similar at a cursory glance, so please read carefully.

central tale'), in an interview where he acknowledged the debt that *Timewyrm: Revelation*'s 'story of a guy going into a dark pit, confronting himself and climbing back out again' owed to Campbell[206].

Campbell's 'monomyth', condensed from a formidable body of world mythology, fairy tale and folklore by the application of Jungian archetypal analysis, was originally presented in *The Hero with a Thousand Faces* (1949), and has since achieved unsurpassed penetration in popular culture. George Lucas used Campbell's model in structuring his original **Star Wars** film trilogy (1977-83)[207], and in the form popularised by Christopher Vogler, author of *The Writer's Journey: Mythic Structure for Storytellers and Screenwriters* (1992)[208], it is now routinely considered in Hollywood and elsewhere as an essential model for storytelling.

The Hero with 13 Faces

Campbell's summary of the monomyth begins with the hero 'setting forth from his commonday hut or castle,'[209] and Vogler emphasises that 'If you're going to show a fish out of his customary element, you first have to show him in that **Ordinary World** to create a vivid contrast with the strange new world he is about to

---

[206] Bishop, David, 'A Conversation with Paul Cornell'.
[207] Larsen, Stephen, and Robin Larsen, *Joseph Campbell: A Fire in the Mind – The Authorized Biography*, p541.
[208] *The Writer's Journey: Mythic Structure For Writers* in later (1998 and 2007) editions. The book grew out of a memo which Vogler wrote in 1985 for Disney, his then employers, and is preserved on his website (Vogler, Christopher 'A Practical Guide to Joseph Campbell's *The Hero with a Thousand Faces*').
[209] Campbell, *Hero*, p245.

enter.'[210] It is true that many of the myths Campbell analyses deal with the adventures of gods or heroes whose routine lives are far from 'ordinary', so this should not be taken as an infallible rule. *Human Nature* [NA] begins with an excerpt from Benny's diaries leading up to the seventh Doctor becoming human, and *Human Nature* [TV] opens with a brief scene of the 10th Doctor in his TARDIS. However, neither displays the characteristic opening moves of the Campbellian 'monomyth', and both quickly transition to a much more 'commonday' setting – albeit one somewhat historically removed from the reader or viewer – where John Smith (his name a byword for ordinariness) lives a mundane, untroubled life before becoming embroiled in adventure. Both stories fit best into Campbell's schema if Smith, rather than the Doctor, is considered their hero, although this is by no means the only angle from which such an analysis might be approached.

What follows is one provisional attempt to align *Human Nature / The Family of Blood* with Campbell's 'Hero's Journey', based on this assumption about the hero's identity. Where *Human Nature* [NA] follows the same outline as its adaptation, additional insights from the novel are included, but no parallel attempt is made to trace Dr John Smith's progression through the book.

Campbell describes the Hero's Journey in 17 stages (split between three broader phases), not all of which are applicable to every myth. Vogler supplies an abridged and altered 12-point version, in which many of Campbell's categories are merged[211]. In what

---

[210] Vogler, Christopher, *The Writer's Journey: Mythic Structure for Storytellers and Screenwriters* p19 (all emphasis in these quotes Vogler's).
[211] Vogler, *The Writer's Journey* p16.

follows we use Vogler's categories, though sometimes with Campbell's names. They are as follows:

Departure

1. The Ordinary World
2. The Call to Adventure
3. The Refusal of the Call
4. The Mentor
5. Crossing the First Threshold

Initiation

6. The Road of Trials
7. The Approach to the Inmost Cave
8. The Supreme Ordeal
9. Seizing the Sword

Return

10. The Road Back
11. Master of Two Worlds
12. Freedom to Live

1. The Ordinary World

Campbell chooses not to emphasise the hero's life before the beginning of their adventure, but Vogler considers this a prerequisite for effective modern storytelling[212].

Accordingly, Smith begins the story as an apparently ordinary schoolteacher, ignorant of his own special status, the danger posed by the imminent arrival of the Family or the coming War. We see him going about a common day:

---

[212] Vogler, *The Writer's Journey* p19.

waking, eating breakfast, teaching, flirting diffidently with Joan. It is confirmed that he is 'as human as they come.'[213]

2. The Call to Adventure[214]

Campbell's archetypal hero begins their journey when they encounter some impetus to leave behind their comfortable world and travel into the unknown.

Campbell notes that 'Typical of the circumstances of the call are the dark forest, the great tree [...] and the loathly, underestimated appearance of the carrier of the power of destiny.'[215] In *Human Nature* [NA], the agent of Smith's call is Benny, who arrives at the school asking for his help, and takes him to find the Pod. She is dressed in 'immodest' jeans and a T-shirt, which scandalise his pupils, and expects to find the Pod in one specific tree in an apple orchard[216].

The equivalent scene in *Human Nature* [TV] is Martha's arrival in Smith's rooms with the panicked revelation that 'They've found us' and her insistence that 'You've got to open the watch'. Neither forest nor tree are present, but Martha is black, a woman and a servant – facts which the other characters are not reticent in commenting on – so is even more 'underestimated' by pre-War society than Benny[217].

---

[213] *Human Nature* [TV].
[214] Campbell, *Hero*, p49; Vogler, *The Writer's Journey* p19.
[215] Campbell, *Hero*, p51-52.
[216] *Human Nature* [NA] pp62-63.
[217] *Human Nature* [TV].

3. The Refusal of the Call[218]

Typically, the hero's initial response to their Call to Adventure is to reject it and continue to embrace the mundane world.

In *Human Nature* [TV] as in *Human Nature* [NA], the repository of the Doctor's Time Lord essence is gone, stolen by Tim. The novel's Smith dismisses Benny's concerns: 'All these... fantasies. They're bad for you. They get between you and the real world'[219]. The TV Smith is even more patronising: 'It must be so confusing for you... Martha, this is what we call a **story**.'[220]

Arguably, the televisual Smith has experienced two previous Calls to Adventure: his recurrent dream of life as the Doctor (Campbell states that the 'zone unknown' to which the hero is called may be 'a profound dream state')[221] and the sighting of the 'meteorite' which is in fact the Family's spaceship. In all three instances, he refuses the opportunity – dismissing his dream as 'just a dream', the spacecraft as 'just rocks falling to the ground', and Martha, after she slaps him, from his service entirely[222].

---

[218] Campbell, *Hero*, p59; Vogler, *The Writer's Journey* p21.
[219] *Human Nature* [NA] pp65-66.
[220] *Human Nature* [TV].
[221] Campbell, *Hero*, p58. The equivalent in *Human Nature* [NA] is a story Dr Smith is writing for his own entertainment, and is more difficult to consider in the light of a Campbellian call.
[222] *Human Nature* [TV].

4. The Mentor

The Mentor is a character who helps to induct the hero into the unknown world. In both versions of Cornell's story, the ostensible relationship between hero and mentor is inverted: the character who teaches Smith is his pupil, Tim, as he himself absorbs the Doctor's values from the Pod or the watch. (This relationship is clearer in *Human Nature* [NA], where Tim has multiple opportunities to impart these insights, than in *Human Nature / The Family of Blood*.) Campbell says that the 'protective figure' is 'often a little old crone or old man'[223], so giving this role to a child is an ironic reversal – although Tim does in fact become an old man by the end of the story.

It is not essential that the story depict the hero's first meeting with the mentor: Vogler observes merely that 'By this time many stories will have introduced a Merlin-like character who is the hero's **Mentor**'[224]. In Campbell's scheme, the scene where the mentor aids the hero follows the latter's rejection of the call, which is not the case in *Human Nature* [TV]. However, the order of events in Campbell's monomyth is subject to variation, and as Vogler says, 'The stages can be deleted, added to, and drastically shuffled without losing any of their power'[225]. This will become relevant again later.

[223] Campbell, *Hero*, p69. Campbell calls this stage 'Supernatural Aid'.
[224] Vogler, *The Writer's Journey* p21.
[225] Vogler, *The Writer's Journey* p30.

In any case, we miss Smith's first meeting with Tim, as the two are in an established teacher-pupil relationship when the story begins. In *Human Nature* [NA], their first significant interaction occurs when Tim gives Smith an apple after a history lesson – a traditional gift to a teacher, but also emblematic of knowledge in the Biblical Garden of Eden story. Since Tim has found the Pod in the apple-tree in the orchard, it is easy to interpret this as representing his handing-on of knowledge[226].

In *Human Nature* [TV], Tim's mentor role is less developed. Their first onscreen encounter prompts Smith's realisation that 'No man should hide himself', while later, in his rejection of the ethos of war in the firing-range scene, Tim begins to put into practice the wisdom he is absorbing from the watch, and provokes the reasoned discussion of military values between Smith and Joan[227]. In neither case, though, does Tim actively impart wisdom to Smith[228].

---

[226] *Human Nature* [NA] p43.
[227] *Human Nature* [TV].
[228] Indeed, in the latter instance it is Joan who does this. An alternative reading might perhaps make Joan Smith's mentor, inducting him into the unfamiliar feminine world of courtship and romance.

5. Crossing the First Threshold[229]

Eventually, willingly or otherwise, the hero must become fully committed to their adventure. The threshold they cross in doing so may be literal or symbolic, and is often patrolled by a guardian of protective and destructive power[230]. Beyond it, the hero enters in a new realm (which Campbell calls 'The Belly of the Whale'), definitively separated from the world they know. This stage therefore concludes the first of the journey's three phases, 'Departure'[231].

In symbolic terms, we might say that Smith in *Human Nature* [TV] crosses his threshold when he casts aside his inhibitions and invites Joan to the dance. Later, though, the couple cross a literal threshold to enter the village hall. The Crimean War veteran is the guardian in this case, his military past symbolising the nature of the adventure Smith will face[232].

6. The Road of Trials

Campbell writes that 'Once having traversed the threshold, the hero moves in a dream landscape of fluid, ambiguous forms, where he must survive a succession of trials.'[233]

---

[229] Vogler, *The Writer's Journey* pp16, 22. This is the stage as defined by Vogler, subsuming into Campbell's 'Crossing the First Threshold' stage its sequel, 'The Belly of the Whale' (Campbell, *Hero*, pp77, 90).
[230] Campbell, *Hero*, pp77, 82.
[231] Or, as Vogler calls it, 'Act One' (*The Writer's Journey* p16).
[232] *Human Nature* [TV].
[233] Campbell, *Hero*, p97.

Vogler divides Campbell's 'Road of Trials' into 'Tests, Allies and Enemies' and 'Approach to the Inmost Cave'. Of the former, he writes that 'Saloons and seedy bars seem to be good places for these transactions' – the hero's trials, and their forging of alliances and enmities – citing Rick's Café in *Casablanca* (1942), the Cantina in *Star Wars* (1977) and the saloon bar in a typical Western[234]. Though more genteel, the village hall – where Smith and Joan are followed by Martha and Tim, and where 'Lucy' observes them and calls her Family to join them – fulfils a parallel function.

Smith's first trial is *Human Nature* [TV]'s cliffhanger, and 'Baines's insistence that he choose between Martha and Joan. The Family certainly fulfil the definition of 'fluid, ambiguous forms', and confusion continues to surround their identities well into *The Family of Blood*.

Smith's challenges continue too, as he returns to the school and attempts to defend it against the Family and the scarecrows, before accepting the wisdom earlier suggested by Tim and now stated outright by Martha: that exposing the boys to war is wrong and that to be truly heroic he must surrender and flee, enabling them to escape[235]. (Again, this moment of choice is clearer in *Human Nature* [NA], where Dr Smith sees one of his pupils killed and in reprisal turns a gun in anger on the attacking Aubertides, but cannot bring himself to fire[236].)

---

[234] Vogler, *The Writer's Journey*, p23.
[235] *The Family of Blood*.
[236] *Human Nature* [NA] p173.

7. The Approach to the Inmost Cave

Vogler considers the Road of Trials' destination, the '**Inmost Cave**', as a separate stage: 'a dangerous place [...] where the object of the quest is hidden,' and therefore achieved[237].

The Cartwright's cottage where Smith, Joan and Martha take shelter in *The Family of Blood* is not a cave (though its stone walls make it more like one than most modern houses), and Joan is correct when she says 'We should be safe here.' Nonetheless, it is still 'a dangerous place'; it is emphasised that Lucy's parents lost their lives there, and it becomes Smith's vantage point for watching the bombardment of the village. Tim delivers the pocket-watch there, fulfilling Smith's quest, such as it has been[238].

8. The Supreme Ordeal

This is Vogler's umbrella term for four of Campbell's stages, which form the central part of the 'Initiation' phase of the journey: 'The Meeting with the Goddess', 'Woman as Temptress', 'Atonement with the Father' and 'Apotheosis'[239]. The hero is united – romantically, sexually or mystically – with an embodiment of womanhood (or alternatively manhood[240]), but may find this relationship an

---

[237] Vogler, *The Writer's Journey*, pp23-24.

[238] *The Family of Blood*.

[239] Vogler, *The Writer's Journey*, pp16, 25; Campbell, *Hero*, pp109, 120, 126, 149.

[240] Though he draws on myths with protagonists of both sexes, Campbell assumes that a male hero is the default, hence the gendered language he uses here. He does observe that, for a female hero, the equivalent mystical union will be with a masculine

impediment to their true goal: an atonement with a divine parental figure which leads to their own elevation to divinity. *The Family of Blood* brings these stages together, not in strict chronological order, in the single sequence in which Smith has to choose whether or not to open the watch, and in its implied outcome.

Campbell observes that 'The ultimate adventure [...] is commonly represented as a mystical marriage of the triumphant hero-soul with the Queen Goddess of the World'[241]. Joan Redfern is neither queen nor goddess, but we do see a marriage between her and Smith, which – though the point is of course partly that it would have been mundane – is 'mystical' in that it forms part of the transcendent vision of the future which they share[242]. Smith's desire to stay with Joan and fulfil this future is a major element of his reluctance to transcend his current state, as predicted by Campbell: 'The seeker of the life beyond life must press beyond her, surpass the temptations of her call'[243].

---

figure (*Hero*, p119), which, while heteronormative, is at least less sexist.

[241] Campbell, *Hero*, p109.

[242] *The Family of Blood*.

[243] Campbell, *Hero*, p122. Vogler notes that 'From the hero's point of view, members of the opposite sex may appear to be **Shapeshifters**, an archetype of change. They seem to shift constantly in form or age, reflecting the confusing and constantly changing aspects of the opposite sex' (Vogler, *The Writer's Journey*, p27). While Joan does display a dual role, changing from her evening clothes to her nurse's uniform at the school, and is seen at

Vogler says of his combined stage that 'This is a critical moment in any story, an Ordeal in which the hero must die or appear to die so that she may be born again'[244] – and indeed we do see Smith die, again as part of this vision.

His rebirth happens offscreen, after Joan asks him, 'What are you going to do?' Though we do not see it, it is clear that Smith opens the watch and becomes the Doctor once more[245]. Insofar as the story contains an equivalent of Campbell's Atonement with the Father, this is it, since (other than perhaps the TARDIS) the Doctor are the only parents Smith has. Like Campbell's hero, Smith must 'open his soul beyond terror to such a degree that he will be ripe to understand [...] the sickening and insane tragedies of this vast and ruthless cosmos,' a description which could certainly apply to the Doctor's worldview[246].

The outcome of this change is 'Apotheosis', becoming a god, which Campbell outlines in terms of the Bodhisattvas of Buddhism. He notes these figures' transcendence of gender, and their renunciation of Nirvana to bring enlightenment to the world left behind[247]. Though the Doctor has always (so far) been coded as masculine – in the 10th Doctor's case, perhaps excessively so – the Bodhisattva's notional

---

different ages in the flashforward, her shapeshifting tendencies are minimal compared with both the women and the men of the Family.

244 Vogler, *The Writer's Journey*, p26.

245 *The Family of Blood*.

246 Campbell, *Hero*, p147.

247 Campbell, *Hero*, pp149-50, 152, 163.

androgyny might relate to the Doctor's functional sexlessness, at least as far as Joan is concerned. As to the second point, a parallel may exist with the Doctor's backstory of leaving the peace and serenity of Gallifrey to aid sentient life across the cosmos.

9. Seizing the Sword

Though Vogler also calls this stage 'Reward', and Campbell 'The Ultimate Boon'[248], 'Seizing the Sword' seems the most apt description of the outcome of the Supreme Ordeal – certainly for Smith, who sees it more as a punishment or curse. It is a stage of assumption into the divine, which Campbell equates with the death of self, mentioning both Jesus's crucifixion and Odin's sacrifice on the World Tree[249]. In storytelling terms, it revolves around an artefact whose possession the hero is now granted: 'a special weapon like a magic sword, or a token like the Grail or some elixir which can heal the wounded land.'[250]

In *The Family of Blood*, this is, again, the contents of the pocket-watch. The story therefore 'shuffles' Campbell's stages so that the Atonement with the Father, Apotheosis and the Ultimate Boon are simultaneous – in fact identical – events.

---

[248] Vogler, *The Writer's Journey*, p26; Campbell, *Hero*, p172.
[249] Campbell, *Hero*, p191.
[250] Vogler, *The Writer's Journey*, p26.

10. The Road Back

What Campbell describes under the four headings of the third phase, 'Return' – 'Refusal of the Return', 'The Magic Flight', 'Rescue from Without', 'The Crossing of the Return Threshold' – Vogler amalgamates into 'The Road Back'[251]. The hero may refuse to return to the mundane world with their 'boon', preferring the magical world that they have discovered; they may be pursued by the guardians of the stolen artefact; they may require guidance or rescue from others; and they must, finally, cross the threshold back into the world they left.

The scene in the Family's spaceship teases us with an apparent Refusal of the Return, as we are led to believe that John Smith has not in fact become the Doctor, and that the Family will therefore go unpunished. This is followed – at speed – by their escape from the exploding vessel, involving a Crossing of a Threshold back to the mundane world, and a Flight in which the Doctor is, if not pursued by, then at least some yards ahead of, the Family[252].

11. Master of Two Worlds[253]

Vogler calls this stage 'Resurrection': 'a second life-and-death moment, almost a replay of the death and rebirth... a kind of final exam for the hero'[254]. In story terms, the

---

[251] Campbell, *Hero*, pp193, 196, 207, 217; Vogler, *The Writer's Journey*, pp16, 27.
[252] *The Family of Blood*.
[253] Campbell, *Hero*, p229.
[254] Vogler, *The Writer's Journey*, pp16, 28.

Doctor's resurrection must be considered to come at the moment in the spaceship when we realise that he has, in fact, returned[255].

By this penultimate stage, however, Campbell's hero has supposedly gained 'Freedom to pass back and forth across the world division, from the perspectives of the apparitions of time to that of the causal deep and back'[256]. This could be seen as describing the Doctor's everyday life, which Smith has gained; indeed, he ferries the Family across this same division, helping them to stop being 'apparitions of time' and instead consigning them, in various and terrible ways, to 'the causal deep'[257].

12. Freedom to Live

What Vogler calls 'Return with the Elixir', Campbell calls 'Freedom to Live' – freedom, specifically, from the fear of change and death[258]. The 'elixir' is a vague quantity, equating to whatever has been gained from the quest (as Campbell puts it, 'The boon that [the hero] brings restores the world'[259]).

The watch, the quest's material object, is handed back to Tim, in whose keeping it eventually helps save Hutchinson's life[260]. If we see Smith as the story's hero, though, the elixir

---

[255] Campbell, *Hero*, pp214-16.
[256] Campbell, *Hero*, p229.
[257] *The Family of Blood*.
[258] Vogler, *The Writer's Journey*, p29; Campbell, *Hero*, p238.
[259] Campbell, *Hero*, p246.
[260] *The Family of Blood*.

in *The Family of Blood* must again be the **contents** of the watch – the Doctor's true nature as a Time Lord and agent of salvation, which Smith's sacrifice has returned to a world imperilled by the lack of it. Between the beginning of *Human Nature* [TV] and the end of *The Family of Blood*, the Doctor has gained nothing. Smith, on the other hand, has gained the freedom of the universe – even if he has lost his identity in the process.

The Mentor's Journey

Alternative interpretations, making less comprehensive but more creative use of Campbell's system, are also available.

Firstly, it is possible – given that Cornell's comments regarding Campbell's influence are almost always joined with mentions of *Superman II* – that he is thinking of his story as a passage in the larger narrative of the Doctor's adventures, in which certain specific stages are relevant, rather than the overall shape of the monomyth. Cornell's remarks about his protagonist giving up or being stripped of various aspects of his personality suggest that his particular interest is in the Road of Trials, where, as Campbell puts it:

> 'The hero [...] discovers and assimilates his opposite (his own unsuspected self) [...] One by one the resistances are broken. He must put aside his pride, his virtue, beauty and life, and bow or submit to the absolutely intolerable. Then he finds that he and his opposite are not of differing species, but one flesh.'

Campbell illustrates this with the Babylonian myth of Inanna's descent into the underworld, in which this process of 'putting aside' is symbolised by the central character being stripped naked. Inanna is yet another deity who hangs on a stake, apparently dead, before being resurrected[261]. Campbell places her resurrection in the Rescue from Without stage of the Hero's Journey[262].

In *Timewyrm: Revelation*, the 'opposite [...] unsuspected self' with whom the seventh Doctor must reconcile is his crucified fifth persona, his moral conscience. In *Human Nature* [NA], and therefore in *Human Nature / The Family of Blood*, the two personas are John Smith and the Doctor.

Freed from the obligation to present the opening and closing stages of Campbell's monomyth, and considered instead as an interpretation of its central episodes, these stories can certainly be seen in terms of the Doctor 'putting aside' his Time Lord 'powers, associations, literary clothes, etc.,' and facing his own humanity. With the Doctor rather than Smith as the hero, they can be read as stories in which the Time Lord enters an unfamiliar world and faces the fallible, mortal aspects of himself – the part of him which can love a woman, fail a child and potentially even fire a gun in anger – before overcoming them and returning, with his strength renewed for his eternal struggle. Most of the stages between the Road of Trials and the Rescue – the Approach to the Inmost Cave, the Meeting with the Goddess, Seizing the Sword – would remain the same as in our previous interpretation, but with Smith seen as an aspect of the Doctor's personality, rather than the hero in his own right.

---

[261] Campbell, *Hero*, pp105-08.
[262] Campbell, *Hero*, pp214-16.

The Doctor is no Master of Two Worlds, however: like Superman, he cannot synthesise his two lives, but must choose one or the other. He cannot be both Time Lord and human; he cannot have both the TARDIS and Joan. While 21st-century **Doctor Who** is cautiously open to the idea of the Doctor's character undergoing gradual development rather than the catastrophic change of regeneration, it would be rare for this to be effected in a story written by someone other than the showrunner. Russell T Davies' 'Lonely God' arc story relies on the 10th Doctor continuing along the same path he has been following since *The Parting of the Ways*, so the wisdom he is able to gain from his time as a human is limited. Ultimately, the weight of the continuing narrative of **Doctor Who** itself forbids the personal enlightenment that the fullest expression of Campbell's monomyth as a single **Doctor Who** story would necessitate.

Alternatively, we might consider the character of the Doctor himself, and in particular his role in the lives of his companions. Perhaps the clearest example of this comes in the final moments of *Rose* (2005):

DOCTOR

What d'you think? You could stay here, fill your life with work and food and sleep, or you could go, er... anywhere.

ROSE

Is it always this dangerous?

DOCTOR

Yeah.

ROSE

Yeah, I can't. I've, um... I've got to go and find my mum, and

PATS MICKEY

someone's got to look after this stupid lump so...

DOCTOR

OK. See you around.

HE STEPS INTO THE TARDIS, WHICH DISAPPEARS.

ROSE

Come on, let's go. Come on. Come on.

ROSE AND MICKEY START TO WALK AWAY. THE TARDIS REAPPEARS AND THE DOCTOR EMERGES.

DOCTOR

By the way, did I mention? It also travels in time.

ROSE

Thanks.

MICKEY

Thanks for what?

ROSE

Exactly.

ROSE KISSES MICKEY BRIEFLY, AND RUNS INTO THE TARDIS WITHOUT LOOKING BACK.

This short scene incorporates four full stages of the Hero's Journey: the Call to Adventure, the Refusal of the Call, Supernatural Aid and the Crossing of the Threshold. Of course, this interpretation necessitates casting Rose in the role of the hero, and the Doctor as her mentor[263].

The Doctor is, in fact, at least as close a match for the Mentor archetype as for the Hero[264]. He is sometimes an old man, and often (as in his fifth or 11th incarnations) remains one in spirit even while appearing young. He is an inventor and a scientist – one of the modern forms taken by the mentor figure according to Vogler, who relates it to the Greek legend of Daedalus[265]. In *Battlefield* (1989) he is even identified directly with Merlin, one of the most immediately recognisable of all mentor characters, and the one Vogler cites as his first example[266].

Vogler writes that 'Mentors represent the self, the god within us... the wiser, nobler, more godlike part of us.' If Tim is Smith's mentor, it is because he stands as a proxy for the Doctor – the 'wiser, nobler, more godlike' part which Smith has had surgically excised. Vogler adds that:

---

[263] Rose's story continues to follow the pattern: *The End of the World* sees her in the Belly of the Whale, separated entirely from her familiar world; in *The Parting of the Ways* she experiences a Meeting with the Goddess and an Apotheosis, and by the time of *The Stolen Earth* (2008) she has become a Master of Two Worlds.

[264] At other times he may represent other Jungian archetypal figures, such as the Trickster or the Wounded Healer.

[265] Vogler, *The Writer's Journey*, p54.

[266] Vogler, *The Writer's Journey*, p21. For more on this, see Appendix 3.

> 'Mentor figures [...] stand for the hero's highest aspirations. They are what the hero may become if she persists [...] Mentors are often former heroes who have survived life's trials and are now passing on the gift of their knowledge and wisdom.'[267]

By this interpretation, Smith moves from being a hero to being a mentor – thanks to the teaching (at one remove) of that very same mentor. Tim eventually gives up his own archetypal role so that Smith can graduate from hero to mentor status.

Though the Doctor routinely acts as a mentor to his companions, inducting them into his alien world, this arrangement is rarely as explicit as in Russell T Davies' scripts[268]. From *Rose* onward it is clear that Davies sees the companion as the protagonist, the Everywoman whose exploration of a new world the viewer follows in much the same way as Campbell's hero[269].

Rose's final scene is paralleled in Martha's introductory episode, *Smith and Jones* (2007). Asked by the Doctor whether she 'might fancy a trip', Martha pleads her academic, financial and family obligations. The Doctor then demonstrates his credentials as a time-traveller by travelling back to that morning – the beginning of the episode, in fact, – and meeting Martha there. On his return, he repeats his invitation and Martha enters the TARDIS[270].

---

[267] Vogler, *The Writer's Journey*, pp51-52.
[268] In the 20th century, the relationship is clearest in the cases of Leela and Ace.
[269] For more on this point, see Chapter 1: in Arnold, Jon, *The Black Archive # 1: Rose* (2016).
[270] *Smith and Jones*.

Unlike Rose, Martha's tenure as a regular companion lasts just one season, and in it many of the plot beats of the Hero's Journey are played out. Martha will experience her own Supreme Ordeal as she wanders an Earth under the dominion of the Master and the Toclafane; she will bring the elixir (ostensibly the Time-Lord-killing gun, but actually the prayers of humanity) which will save the Doctor and thus the world; and she will Cross the Return Threshold when she leaves the TARDIS to take up a professional role as a doctor in her own right[271]. When we see her again, she is able to transition easily between the mundane and alien worlds[272].

Her Supreme Ordeal happens, however, in the absence of the Doctor, who is imprisoned – and aged beyond human tolerances – by the Master[273]. Although it is not a defined stage of Campbell's Hero's Journey, it is highly characteristic of mentors that they leave their proteges alone to face their most dangerous trials. Obi-Wan Kenobi is struck down by Darth Vader[274]; Gandalf is banished into the deeps by the Balrog[275]; Merlin is imprisoned eternally by a sorceress[276]. As Vogler puts it, 'the mentor can only go so far with the hero. Eventually the hero must face the unknown alone.'[277] Sometimes they return, transfigured: Obi-Wan becomes more powerful than Vader can possibly imagine; Gandalf returns from the abyss as Gandalf the White; the Doctor regains not only his

---

[271] *Last of the Time Lords.*
[272] *The Sontaran Stratagem / The Poison Sky* (2008).
[273] *Last of the Time Lords.*
[274] *Star Wars.*
[275] Tolkein, JRR, *The Lord of the Rings* (1954-55).
[276] This tradition, alluded to in *Battlefield*, probably dates back to mediaeval French romances.
[277] Vogler, *The Writer's Journey*, p22.

youth but (briefly) the ability to levitate, move objects telekinetically, resist laser blasts and glow[278].

Even so, when Martha faces her own Supreme Ordeal, it is without the Doctor, just as she is without him throughout most of *Human Nature / The Family of Blood*. In *Human Nature* [TV] this makes her feel helpless, as she twice turns, equally fruitlessly, to his recording for advice: 'What am I supposed to do then? [...] I wish you'd come back.' In *The Family of Blood* she takes the initiative. Smith fails the test at the village hall, but Martha passes it, successfully getting herself, Smith and Joan safely away from the Family.

If we were to see Martha as a Campbellian hero, and the 2007 season of **Doctor Who** as her journey, then *Human Nature / The Family of Blood* would be a trial run for her forthcoming loss of her mentor, her own heroism in his absence, and his eventual triumphant return.

'It's Silly, That's All. Just Stories.'

The two-part TV story can, therefore, be fitted with a reasonable degree of accuracy into the format of Campbell's monomyth, whether we take the protagonist to be John Smith, the Doctor or Martha. However, the usefulness of such a reading is questionable for a number of reasons.

Firstly, Campbell's work is descriptive, not prescriptive – indeed, it reads at times like a work of mystical meditation upon the numinous, rather than a serious academic investigation. It does not appear that he intended to write a template for future story-creation: rather, he was describing patterns into which the stories

[278] *Last of the Time Lords*.

which human beings tell will tend naturally to fall. Indeed, George Lucas states that he began plotting *Star Wars* **before** reading *The Hero with a Thousand Faces*, and found it 'eerie' how closely his ideas mirrored Campbell's outline[279].

As disciples like Lucas and Vogler have spread awareness of Campbell's work, especially among creators of visual media, such patterns have become perhaps more deeply ingrained in Western narrative than at earlier times in history. In this light, it is relatively unsurprising that a work of 21st-century visual media like *Human Nature / The Family of Blood* should fit so easily into Vogler's simplified version of Campbell's schema[280].

Furthermore, Campbell's stages – especially as interpreted through Vogler's somewhat reductive and utilitarian formula – are very general and widely applicable; perhaps so much so that, with the necessary confirmation bias, almost any story might be seen to fit them. (As if to illustrate this point, the second edition of *The Writer's Journey* includes a detailed 'Hero's Journey' interpretation of various films including *Four Weddings and a Funeral* (1994)[281].) Not only can the elements of the Hero's Journey be 'shuffled', but non-linear aspects may be slotted in according to either narrative or diegetic chronology, and the hero role shifted from character to character, to fit the scheme better. (We might, for instance, have analysed the story from Tim's or Joan's point of view, or

---

[279] Larsen and Larsen, *Joseph Campbell*, p541.
[280] There are certainly a number of other **Doctor Who** stories that at least partially fit this scheme: prior to *Rose*, the regeneration stories *Planet of the Spiders* (1974), *Logopolis* (1981) and *The Caves of Androzani* all spring to mind as apt examples.
[281] Vogler, *The Writer's Journey*, pp296-306.

incorporated the flashback to the Doctor's metamorphosis as a Crossing of the First Threshold.) Ultimately, to say that a particular story can, from a specific perspective, appear to fit into a very general description of the characteristics of stories, is an observation so trivial it borders on the banal.

Cornell has of course spoken explicitly of Campbell's influence, and we should take him at his word. However, to say that one is inspired by a work of narratology is a very different thing from saying that one is inspired by a specific story. What Cornell does with the mythologies of Jesus, Odin and the Doctor in *Timewyrm: Revelation* may well have emerged from Campbell's work showing him how they might be used, but its interest and its power derive from the disparate legends themselves, and the way they are combined. Equally, modern cinema's insistence on creating Campbell-inflected narratives by imposing Vogler's formula on films such as *Star Trek* (2009) or *Man of Steel* (2013) – to name just two brought to mind by Cornell's inspirations for *Human Nature* [NA] – has not ineluctably imbued them with thematic profundity.

Human Nature / The Family of Blood has much to tell us – about war, childhood, family, racism, class, history and human nature itself – but this derives from the specifics of Cornell's engagement with the world, culture and people surrounding him, not from his obedience to a formula deemed to represent good storytelling. And ultimately, the story's value **as a story** comes from what makes it unique, not what makes it like every other story ever told.

CONCLUSION

In Chapter 5, we discussed the 'Crossing of the Threshold' phase of the Hero's Journey in terms of Smith and Joan's arrival at the Village Hall. However, it would be more accurate to say that *Human Nature / The Family of Blood* is full of thresholds.

As we have observed, the boarding-school is an ambiguous space populated by human beings who are neither children nor adults. Within it, Smith's rooms, and his thoughts, are shared between his waking and his dream lives. The threshold of the pub may be crossed by men but not by women. The Family's spaceship is a place of transformation where the human becomes the alien. The cottage where Smith must decide his path is poised between his ordinary human life and his lordship of time. Tim's rescue of Hutchinson apparently takes place between the English and German lines, in the supremely liminal territory of 'No Man's Land'.

The TARDIS – the entering of which kickstarts the story – is perhaps the ultimate threshold, a doorway whose crossing may lead to any time, any world, or any genre of narrative.

And *Human Nature / The Family of Blood* occupies a boundary space of its own. A decade-old TV story which owes its conception, its structure and its themes to a two-decade-old novel, it is neither wholly a product of early-21st-century TV **Doctor Who** nor of the 1990s **New Adventures**. It navigates the borders between literary and televisual **Doctor Who**, as its characters do those between war and peace, school and family, mortality and divinity, humanity and alienness.

Across this threshold, ideas from the novels are imported into the TV series. It is true that the mysticism characteristic of the **New Adventures** has remained largely absent since, except occasionally in specific stories such as *In the Forest of the Night* (2014) or *The Eaters of Light* (2017). The adaptation is also only partially successful in importing the **New Adventures**' politics, abstaining from *Human Nature* [NA]'s radical pacifism in favour of deploring war within more conventional parameters. (It does, however, introduce explicit depiction of real-world racism to the 21st-century TV series – for the first time since the **New Adventures** precursor *Remembrance of the Daleks* – to be revisited as recently as *Thin Ice* (2017)[282].)

The story's central conceit has had more influence, however, at least while Russell T Davies remained in charge of the series. While a determined showrunner would always have found some way to restore the Master to a universe supposedly bereft of Time Lords, the actual mechanism chosen in *Utopia* has the Doctor's archenemy, like the Doctor himself, becoming human – and Professor Yana's personality offers us insights into the Master's character in the same way John Smith's has to the Doctor's. By the

---

[282] While the 21st-century series has largely been content to counter racism implicitly (by depicting matter-of-fact acceptance of ethnic diversity, including in historical periods) and through allegorical parallels (for instance, by reiterating the Daleks' well-established hatred of the other), it is significant that Martha and Bill specifically are given the opportunity to react to the kinds of prejudice people of colour encounter in mundane present-day reality, albeit in both cases projected into the historical past.

end of the 2008 season, the Doctor is seen to have literally split into two selves, one of them human[283].

The story's influence on the Doctor himself, within the narrative, is equally explicit. During the farewell montage which follows the instigating events of his regeneration in *The End of Time*, but precedes the regeneration proper, the only person he visits who is not a former companion – or, in fact, a character whom we have seen before – is Joan's great-granddaughter, Verity Newman, who is signing a book she has based on Joan's diaries. While the emotional impact of the scene is enhanced significantly by the fact that Verity, like Joan, is played by Jessica Hynes, it is David Tennant's reaction when she asks the Doctor whether he was 'happy, in the end' that convinces the viewer that the end of their relationship is one of the greatest regrets of this lifetime[284].

Though *Human Nature / The Family of Blood* is not the first time on TV that the Doctor has had what appears to be a romance – *Doctor Who* (1996) and *The Girl in the Fireplace* (2006) are the obvious precedents – it represents the first love-affair that is shown to have had a lasting impact on him, and paves the way for the arrival of River Song in *Silence in the Library / Forest of the Dead*, and her history with the 11th and 12th Doctors thereafter. It is in this vulnerability to the longer-term effects of love, rather than in the romance itself, that the lingering effects of the 10th Doctor's briefly-enjoyed humanity are most clearly seen[285].

---

[283] *Journey's End*.

[284] *The End of Time* episode 2.

[285] Even in the absence of its many sequels, the clear implication of *Silence in the Library / Forest of the Dead* is that River and the

Though we have spoken at length of how Smith's humanness is contrasted with the Doctor's habitual Time Lordly character, this book has had relatively little to say about what *Human Nature / The Family of Blood* tells us of 'human nature' itself. To judge by how human beings act in the story, a major aspect of this is yet another dichotomy, embracing but extending beyond that relating to war and peace. It stands between, on the one hand, the self-centred ignorance which results in Hutchinson's bullying of Tim, Rocastle's bellicosity, Joan's racism and Smith's acceptance of all of these as normal; and on the other the selflessness and empathy that give us Tim's forgiveness of Hutchinson, Rocastle's concern for 'Lucy', and ultimately Joan and Smith's altruistic sacrifice of their future happiness.

A humanistic outlook would suggest that, for each of these divisive categories, both sides fall within the remit of what it means to be human, and that our natures include both the best and the worst of what humanity can be; that we necessarily exist in 'the place where the falling angel meets the rising ape'[286]. The implication is that, since we are capable of both great good and great evil, we should strive for the former. By giving the Doctor the opportunity to explore his imperfect human nature, the story allows us to see our own nature reflected, and inspires us to appreciate its importance.

Doctor's relationship lies in the future. Had it been River rather than (by proxy) Joan whom the Doctor revisited in *The End of Time* episode 2, the impact would have been a great deal less elegiac and valedictory.

[286] Terry Pratchett, *Hogfather* p270.

APPENDIX 1: CHECKLIST OF CHARACTER EQUIVALENCES

Human Nature [NA]	***Human Nature / The Family of Blood***	**Notes**
The seventh Doctor	**The 10th Doctor**	A different incarnation, his personality established in prior stories.
Dr John Smith	**Mr John Smith**	Not Scottish. More consistently a man of his time rather than an outlier in it.
Bernice Summerfield		Replaced with **Martha**.
	Martha Jones	Personality established in prior stories. Poses as a domestic servant rather than Smith's niece.
Mrs Joan Redfern	**Nurse Joan Redfern**	School matron rather than science teacher. Widow of Oliver, not Arthur, Redfern.
Tim Dean	**Tim Latimer**	Naturally psychic. No longer identifies closely with the stored persona of the Doctor.

***Human Nature* [NA]**	***Human Nature / The Family of Blood***	**Notes**
The Aubertides:	**The Family of Blood:**	Similar in broad motivation, but with different origins, biology and personalities. No names.
	• **'Baines'**	New character.
	• **'Mr Clark'**	New character.
• August		No TV equivalent.
• Greeneye	• **'Jenny'** (See also **Jenny**)	Takes the form of the companion's friend; otherwise, a new character.
• Serif		No TV equivalent.
• Laylock		No TV equivalent.
• Aphasia	• **'Lucy Cartwright'**	Similar in appearance, but not in character.
• Hoff		No TV equivalent.

***Human Nature* [NA]**	***Human Nature / The Family of Blood***	**Notes**
Mr Rocastle	**Mr Rocastle**	Reduced role. No longer romantically interested in Joan. His death is now misguided.
Hutchinson	**Hutchinson**	Radically reduced role. Survives the War.
Alexander Shuttleworth		No TV equivalent.
Richard Hadleman		No TV equivalent; Tim instead saves Hutchinson during the War.
Constance Harding	**Jenny** (See also **'Jenny'**)	The companion's friend and confidante, with whom she discusses women's rights.
Anand		No TV equivalent. (Martha inherits some of the racism he experiences.)
Clive Ian Alton		No TV equivalent. (The character is revealed as a Time Lord intelligence agent, so would have no parallel in this era of the series.)

APPENDIX 2: BUT CAN'T MAYFLIES BREED?

> 'The Doctor said the Family's got a limited lifespan, and that's why they need to consume a Time Lord. Otherwise, three months and they die. Like mayflies, he said.'
>
> [Martha, *The Family of Blood*]

In Chapter 3 we suggested that the species to which the Family of Blood belongs, being individually short-lived, would tend to prioritise the aims and concerns of the family over those of its individual members. This raises an important question, however: how can the Doctor be so sure that their three-month lifespan will determine how long they come after him? Surely, if pursuing the Time Lord has become a family goal, it could potentially be passed down from parent to child for many generations – years, at least?

A possible answer lies in the fact that the Family have pursued the Doctor to Earth through time and space from an unknown location[287]. They use terms for kinship which are equivalent to those in (Anglophone) human culture – 'mother', 'father', 'son', 'daughter', 'sister', 'husband' and 'wife' are all heard during the course of the episodes – so they may follow humanlike taboos

[287] The fact that 'Baines' knows of the coming War might imply that they come from 1913's future. However, he also says that they have 'travelled far and wide looking for Mr Smith,' which could alternatively imply that they have visited the future but do not originate there.

against breeding with close relatives[288]. This being the case, a short lifespan would normally compel a family to remain in close contact with the species' main population centres, to ensure available breeding stock for the always-imminent next generation.

It may be that, in following the Doctor, the Family have removed themselves too far from such centres – either in space (if the nearest centre is months or more away by spaceflight) or in time (since an individually short-lived species would be subject to rapid genetic change, any of its members existing in 1913 may be genetically incompatible with those from the Family's home era). If it is also the case that its older generation are too old to produce further offspring, this would leave the Family as a whole functionally sterile unless it resorts to endogamy.

However, this explanation relies on the Family being unable to reuse their stolen vortex manipulator – otherwise there is nothing to prevent one of the younger generation nipping back to their home location and era, finding a mate and having children there, and then returning with them to Earth in 1913[289].

Furthermore, the Doctor's confidence regarding the time limit relies on his being aware of all these obstacles – social, biological and practical.

---

[288] This raises the question of whether they choose to inhabit specific hosts based on their perceived ages and genders, to mimic the existing relationships.

[289] There is no reason to assume that the fact that 'Lucy' is occupying the body of a small girl means that she is herself too young to breed. Even if she is, it can surely only be a matter of weeks before she attains sexual maturity.

This appears to be an example of an attempt to fix a plot hole in the original version of the story resulting in a new plot hole in the adaptation. A need to hide (even though it turns out in the end to be a **preference** to hide, rather than to inflict punishment on his hunters) gives the 10th Doctor a stronger motivation to become human than the seventh Doctor's whim – but the story's logic as stated would require him to hide indefinitely, until the Family's future generations died out or lost interest.

(Another possible solution might be that the species does not, in fact, enjoy the kind of cultural continuity we have envisaged, with grandchildren instead regularly and reliably rejecting the values of their grandparents – but on such short timescales this would make for a profoundly unstable society, and we see no hint of clashing priorities in the interactions between the present-day members of the Family. Besides, unless their cultural memory is similarly short, there would be nothing to stop some distant future generation of the Family – perhaps three or four years' hence – from rediscovering and enthusiastically embracing their ancestors' purpose.)

In the TV story, the Family want the Doctor's DNA so they can become immortal (or at least relatively so), replacing the months of their own lifespans with the millennia of a Time Lord's. In the source novel, the Aubertide family Dubraxine are intending to overcome a different biological cap, on their reproductive capabilities. Each 'family' of Aubertides is produced by asexual budding from a single individual (originally conceived sexually by the Aubertide King and Queen[290]), but this budding is possible for

[290] *Human Nature* [NA] p163.

only six 'generations'. The family Dubraxine hope that, by assimilating Time Lord biodata, they will become able to regenerate, budding once more with each new incarnation to produce offspring with the same abilities, and thus reproducing exponentially[291].

The Aubertide lifespan is longer than that of the Family of Blood, but still limited: the Doctor suggests that Greeneye, the second oldest, has, 'what, ten more years at the most? That's the thing about such powerful biosystems. They burn themselves out.'[292]. This would mean that, if the seventh Doctor had somehow remained as Smith for a given number of decades, his pursuers would have died out without being replaced by a new generation, and he would have been free to resume life as a Time Lord, unmolested (at least by them). A similar combination of limitations – together with the TV episodes' amendment to the antagonists' lifespan – could plausibly give the 10th Doctor his sentence of three months' humanity, but no such restriction on the Family's ability to breed is stated.

The answer, then, to the question 'Why can't the Family chase the Doctor indefinitely?', would appear to be authorial fiat – or at least a plot point that has been lost in the transition between novel and TV episodes. We might interpolate a backstory where the Family, like their Aubertide forebears, have been exiled from their home civilisation for their crimes and are therefore cut off from all possibility of producing further progeny, leaving immortality as

---

[291] *Human Nature* [NA] pp129-31.
[292] *Human Nature* [NA] p252.

their only recourse if the Family is to survive. But there is no hint of such a rationale onscreen.

APPENDIX 3: MERLIN THE MENTOR

As observed in Chapter 5, Christopher Vogler in *The Writer's Journey* not only mentions Merlin as a mentor figure, he considers him a touchstone by for identifying such figures ('a Merlin-like character who is the hero's **Mentor**'[293]). In *Battlefield*, one of the TV **Doctor Who** stories which preceded and strongly influenced the Virgin **New Adventures**, the Doctor is directly identified as Merlin, and the plot rests on the idea that he will, at some point in his future, become King Arthur's mentor.

Cornell writes:

> 'Post-*Battlefield*, I really took up the theme of the Doctor as Merlin, and followed the parallels as far as they went. For instance, the wink in the title sequence echoes Merlin's (and many other mythological heroes') loss of an eye to gain wisdom.'[294]

The claim about Merlin's eye is one that Cornell (or his co-writers) have repeated elsewhere[295]. We have been unable to find a source for it outside Cornell's own work, though the legend is certainly told of Odin[296]. In other respects, though, *Human Nature* [NA] creates a parallel with Merlin that carries a similar resonance to

---

[293] Vogler, *The Writer's Journey* p21.

[294] Cornell, Notes to Chapter 7, *Human Nature* [NA], ebook, p351. The **Doctor Who** title sequence introduced in 1987 and used until 1989 shows Sylvester McCoy winking his left eye, though this predates *Battlefield* by two years.

[295] Cornell, Day and Topping, *The Discontinuity Guide* p348.

[296] *Gylfaginning* chapter 15, Sturlson, Snorri, *The Prose Edda*, ed and trans Jesse L Byock, p24.

Timewyrm: Revelation's with Odin. Visited by a symbolic owl (associated with the Time Lords in the **New Adventures**, Cornell's novels in particular), Smith playfully addresses it as 'Merlin', and he later says, summarising what he has learned of the Doctor, that 'He's Merlin. You know the sort of thing.'[297] Early in the book Benny is moved by a reading of Thomas Malory's *Le Morte D'Arthur*, and the later chapters quote from John Boorman's film *Excalibur* (1981)[298].

Joseph Campbell illustrates the final stage of his Hero's Journey, 'Freedom to Live', with a passage from 'The Tale of Taliesin', an account of the legendary Welsh bard of that name, as first written down in the 17th century. For Campbell, the extensive litany of past deeds to which Taliesin implausibly lays claim are those of 'the Imperishable', the eternal spirit which is expressed not only in the bard himself but in all great endeavourers: a hero, in fact, with 1,000 faces. Many of Taliesin's claims have a distinctly Doctorish sound to them:

> '"I know the names of the stars from north to south;
> I have been on the galaxy at the throne of the Distributor [...]
> I have been teacher to all intelligences,
> I am able to instruct the whole universe.

[297] Cornell, *Human Nature* [NA] pp88, 203.
[298] Cornell, *Human Nature* [NA] pp35-36; *Human Nature* [NA], ebook, p356.

> I shall be until the day of doom on the face of the earth [...]"'[299]

In *Human Nature* [NA] Tim Dean quotes another Welsh poem credited to Taliesin, 'Cad Goddeu' ('The Battle of the Trees'), evidently under the influence of the Pod: '"I lived as a warrior before I was a man of letters. I wandered, I encircled, I slept in a hundred islands, I dwelt in a hundred forts."'[300] Though they are occasionally conflated in modern retellings, in most early sources Taliesin is considered as a separate character from Merlin[301]. Contrary to this, however, Cornell states that the Cad Goddeu is 'attributed to Merlin'[302].

For his source in identifying the bard with the wizard, we need look no further than the lines quoted by Campbell, which begin as follows (emphasis ours):

> '"Primary chief bard am I to Elphin,
> And my original country is the region of the summer stars;
> Idno and Heinin **called me Merddin**,

---

[299] Campbell, *Hero*, pp241-43. Campbell quotes from the version included in Lady Charlotte Guest's translation of the Welsh story-cycle *The Mabinogion*.

[300] *Human Nature* [NA] pp123. These lines come from Patrick K Ford's 1977 translation of *The Mabinogion*, so could not possibly be known to Tim in this form in 1914.

[301] Much of Geoffrey of Monmouth's *Vita Merlini* (12th century), for instance, consists of a dialogue between Merlin and Taliesin, who is said to have helped the wizard ferry King Arthur's body to Avalon after his defeat in battle. By contrast, in Marion Zimmer Bradley's *The Mists of Avalon* (1983) 'Merlin' is a title held at different times by different individuals, of whom Taliesin is one.

[302] Notes to Chapter 9, *Human Nature* [NA], ebook, p351.

At length every king will call me Taliesin.”’[303]

Campbell considers the extract as a series of examples of the Imperishable as expressed through the hero after his quest has been fulfilled. This means that rather than being literally the same person as ‘Merddin’, Taliesin may be identifying himself as an avatar of the same spirit who was once Merlin. This is, to say the least, relevant to Tim’s situation as he assimilates aspects of the Doctor’s character from the Pod or, in the television story, the pocket-watch.

---

[303] Campbell, *Hero*, p241. ‘Merddin’ is a variant form of ‘Merlin’.

APPENDIX 4: DID BOTH VERSIONS HAPPEN?

As discussed in our Introduction, for the five years between the publication of John Peel's *Timewyrm: Genesys* in June 1991 and the broadcast of *Doctor Who* in May 1996, the Virgin **New Adventures** represented the contemporary continuing story of **Doctor Who**. Taking up the narrative from the point where 1989's final story, *Survival*, left off, they developed the seventh Doctor's personality, gave him new companions and new enemies, created new recurring characters and revisited old ones; they established their own reasonably coherent continuity, including a broad outline of humanity's future history and of the Doctor's own mysterious past; they even determined the narrative direction of the one other outlet for new **Doctor Who** stories at the time, *Doctor Who Magazine*'s (DWM's) comic strips[304]. They did, in short, everything one might have expected of the TV series, had it not been placed on indefinite hold in 1989[305].

---

[304] Certainly from *Pureblood* (DWM #193-196, cover dates November 1992 to February 1993) to *Cuckoo* (DWM #208-10, cover dates January to March 1994), during which time Benny appears as a regular character.

[305] The most significant difference, other than the obvious one of medium, was that from June 1994 Virgin also published **Missing Adventures** featuring past Doctors, so that this contemporary continuity could – and very frequently did – cross over into the Doctor's ostensible past. This was something that had rarely been seen in the TV series, but was in keeping with, for example, the approach of *The Two Doctors*.

With the broadcast of *Doctor Who* (1996), and the BBC's decision that year not to renew Virgin Publishing's licence to publish **Doctor Who** books, this changed. Though often written by former **New Adventures** authors, the new novels from BBC Books paid only sporadic attention to Virgin continuity, while the later DWM comics[306], and the **Doctor Who** audio dramas which Big Finish Productions began releasing with *The Sirens of Time* in 1999, were not infrequently blasé about contradicting it.

The first half of the 1990s remain a unique period in **Doctor Who**'s history: a time when the series had definite and singular momentum independent of the TV medium. For those viewers with long enough memories and the necessary history, both *Human Nature* [NA] and *Human Nature / The Family of Blood* might therefore be considered as separate episodes in the history of the same character – a 10th Doctor whose own backstory may or may not include some of the eighth Doctor comics, novels or audios[307], but certainly includes the seventh Doctor's **New Adventures**.

Of course, even if there had still been a single definitive body of non-televisual **Doctor Who** in 2005, it would hardly have served Russell T Davies' plans to give the revived series popular appeal if he had explicitly followed a history established only in the minds of the specialist fan viewer. The 21st-century series has made glancing

---

[306] Which made their statement in *Ground Zero* (DWM #238-42, cover dates May to August 1996), by giving Ace a death not easily reconcilable with her **New Adventures** appearances.

[307] Although six years after *Human Nature / The Family of Blood*, 'The Night of the Doctor' (2013) confirmed that the last of these, at least, still occurred within the TV Doctor's history.

reference at best to the Virgin books[308] – with the exception, of course, of *Human Nature / The Family of Blood*. Yet, as an adaptation of the novel in a new medium, this story could rather be seen as a direct **contradiction** of its original. The question of how the Doctor can experience what is essentially the same sequence of events and apparently not notice is one which might prove vexing, to say the least, for those who desire an internally consistent narrative.

Attempting to reconcile apparent inconsistencies, often with increasingly complex justifications, is a pastime that has entertained fans of **Doctor Who** for many years – leading, for instance, to the publication of Lance Parkin and Lars Pearson's monumental *AHistory: An Unauthorised History of Doctor Who* (2006)[309]. Paul Cornell has implied that this particular incongruity might be explained away by damage caused to history and causality

---

[308] The Butler Institute building from Andrew Cartmel's *Cat's Cradle: Warhead* (1992) is visible in *The Poison Sky*, and the Chelonians from Gareth Roberts' *The Highest Science* (1993) are namechecked in *The Pandorica Opens* (2010). (An apparent reference in *Bad Wolf* to the planet Lucifer, the setting of Andy Lane and Jim Mortimore's *Lucifer Rising* (1993), is inconclusive, given that the name is that of a significant figure in mythology – indeed, the novel's title itself quotes Arthur C Clarke's *2010: Odyssey Two* (1982).)

[309] Later republished in second and third editions (2007, 2012), with a supplement in 2014 and a companion volume (*Unhistory: Apocryphal Stories Too Strange Even for Ahistory*) in 2017, *Ahistory* is a revision of Parkin's earlier *Doctor Who: A History of the Universe* (1996), itself an expansion of 'The Doctor Who Chronology' published in the fanzine *Seventh Door* in 1994.

by the Time War[310], but such a general-purpose explanation, which might apply to any inconsistency, is less interesting than the kind of specific reconciliations that Parkin and Pearson offer.

To begin with, we can dismiss the idea that the 10th Doctor says he has never been human before. His comment that he has 'Never used this... all the times I've wondered...' refers explicitly to the Chameleon Arch. Nor is it difficult to explain why the seventh Doctor chose to visit a genetic engineer rather than use the Arch – the process the 10th Doctor undergoes in haste is apparently far more painful[311].

In fact the main issue of credibility lies not in their precise differences between the versions of the story, but in their similarities. The parallels in the broad outline of the plot are excusable – Joseph Campbell aside, **Doctor Who** often deals in stock situations and plot formulae, and it is hardly unusual for the Doctor to end up defending an enclosed community from attacking monsters – but the equivalences in detail are more difficult to explain. In becoming human on two separate occasions, the Doctor apparently ends up twice hiding from a family of aliens by teaching at a boarding-school shortly before the First World War, taking the name John Smith, working for a headmaster named Rocastle, teaching boys called Tim and Hutchinson, and falling in love with a woman named Joan Redfern. Even if the schools have different

[310] Cornell, Paul, 'Canonicity in Doctor Who'.
[311] *Human Nature* [TV].

names[312], the women different occupations and the Tims different surnames, the coincidence still beggars belief.

If we want to reconcile the stories, we must therefore assume that it is not a coincidence[313]. The 10th Doctor tells Martha that 'the TARDIS will take care of everything – invent a life story for me, find me a setting and integrate me.'[314] We must suppose that the TARDIS remembers the previous occasion when the Doctor became human, calculates on this basis that a rural boarding-school shortly before the outbreak of the First World War will be a survivable 'setting', and does its best to maximise the similarities between this and the previous situation. Apparently such details as Joan's profession are not within the TARDIS's control, but the names are no more a coincidence than the recurrence of the phrase 'Bad Wolf' in diverse settings across space and time during the 2005 series.

On that occasion the words were placed by Rose, using the power at the heart of the TARDIS to restructure history on a cultural-linguistic level. Clearly the same ability of the TARDIS is at work here – ensuring that Joan's parents named her 'Joan' and that her husband's ancestors acquired the surname 'Redfern'; arranging for

---

[312] In *Human Nature* [NA], Hulton College School is located near Farringham village (pp21, 15). In *Human Nature / The Family of Blood*, the village goes unnamed, but the school appears (judging by the blurry view of the sign following *Human Nature* [TV]'s opening credits sequence) to be called 'Farringham School for Boys'.

[313] This is Parkin and Pearson's second option ('Both happened and it's not a coincidence'), though the details are ours (*Ahistory*, third edition, pp173-74).

[314] *Human Nature* [TV].

two separate Anglo-Saxon villages to be named as 'the settlement of Fera's people', and so forth, in order to create as many similarities as possible between the Doctor's present situation and this incident from his history.

The only question remaining, then, is why the 10th Doctor would not remember the previous incident, and use this knowledge to predict what might happen should he choose to become human in this context. (Smith, of course, remembers nothing of the Doctor's earlier exploits except in his dreams, so would experience mild déjà vu at most.) One possible explanation might be that these memories have been lost during one of the various times where the Doctor has suffered amnesia or memory loss about his prior life history, leaving him free to experience them 'for the first time' once more[315].

Another would be that the Doctor **does** remember the events of *Human Nature* [NA], but fails to predict the lengths the TARDIS will go to in order to replicate his previous experiences: as far as he is concerned, he might end up in any era or setting. Nor are his similar responses inevitable, even in a parallel setting: the seventh Doctor specifically states that if he were to become human again, he would not be the same John Smith[316], and perhaps the 10th Doctor sees no reason to suppose that a new John Smith would behave in the same way. Perhaps his refusal to countenance the idea that he might fall in love again is yet another form of denial.

---

[315] For example – if we extend the assumption of relevance from the **New Adventures** to the BBC Books **Eighth Doctor Adventures** range – the extended plotline beginning with *The Burning* (2000).
[316] *Human Nature* p257.

In any case, by the time he is himself again, and discovers that during his blackout he has once again had a doomed love-affair in pre-War England, he has too much else on his mind to spend time commenting on the parallels.

BIBLIOGRAPHY

Books

Arnold, Jon, *Rose*. **The Black Archive** #1. Edinburgh, Obverse Books, 2016. ISBN 9781909031371.

The Bible, King James Version. 1611. Oxford, Oxford University Press, 1997. ISBN 9780192835253.

Bunyan, John, *The Pilgrim's Progress*. 1678. London, Penguin Classics, 2009. ISBN 9780141439716.

Bradley, Marion Zimmer. *The Mists of Avalon*. 1982. London, Penguin Books, 1993. ISBN 9780140177190.

Burk, Graeme and Robert Smith?, *Who Is the Doctor: The Unofficial Guide to Doctor Who – The New Series*. Toronto, ECW Press, 2012. ISBN 9781550229844.

Campbell, Joseph, *The Hero with a Thousand Faces*. 1949. London, Fontana Press, 1993. ISBN 9780586085714.

Cornell, Paul, *Timewyrm: Revelation*. **Doctor Who: The New Adventures**. London, Virgin Publishing Ltd, 1991. ISBN 9780426203605.

Cornell, Paul, *Love and War*. **Doctor Who: The New Adventures**. London, Virgin Publishing Ltd, 1992. ISBN 9780426203858.

Cornell, Paul, *Human Nature*. **Doctor Who: The New Adventures**. London, Virgin Publishing Ltd, 1995. ISBN 9780426204435.

Cornell, Paul, *Human Nature*. 1995. **Doctor Who: The History Collection**. BBC Books edition, London, Penguin Random House, 2015. ISBN 9781849909099.

Cornell, Paul, *Happy Endings*. **Doctor Who: The New Adventures**. London, Virgin Publishing Ltd, 1995. ISBN 9780426204701.

Cornell, Paul, *Chalk: A Novel*. New York, Tor.com, 2017. ISBN 9780765390950.

Cornell, Paul, Martin Day and Keith Topping, *Doctor Who: The Discontinuity Guide*. London, Virgin Publishing, 1995. ISBN 9780426204428.

Crome, Andrew and James McGrath, eds, *Time and Relative Dimensions in Faith: Religion and Doctor Who*. London, Darton, Longman and Todd Ltd, 2013. ISBN 9780232530216.

> Charlton, Michael, 'The Doctor Working on God's Time: Kairos and Intervention in *The Waters of Mars* and *A Christmas Carol*'.
>
> Wardley, K Jason, 'Divine and Human Nature: Incarnation and Kenosis in **Doctor Who**'.

David, Peter, *Imzadi*. **Star Trek: The Next Generation**. 1992. New York, Pocket Books, 1993. ISBN 9780671867294.

Davies, Russell T, *Damaged Goods*. **Doctor Who: The New Adventures**. London, Virgin Publishing Ltd, 1996. ISBN 9780426204831.

Davies, Russell T, et al, *Doctor Who: The Shooting Scripts*. London, BBC Books, 2005. ISBN 9780563486411.

Dearmer, Percy, and Ralph Vaughan Williams, eds, *The English Hymnal*. Oxford, Oxford University Press, 1906.

Dicks, Terrance, and Malcolm Hulke, *The Making of Doctor Who*. London, W H Allen, 1976. ISBN 9780426116158.

Driscoll, Paul, *The God Complex*. **The Black Archive** #9. Edinburgh, Obverse Books, 2017. ISBN 9781909031401.

Eliot, TS, *The Complete Poems and Plays of TS Eliot*. London, Faber & Faber, 1969.

Ford, Patrick K, trans, *The Mabinogi and Other Medieval Welsh Tales*. Berkeley and Los Angeles, University of California Press, 1977. ISBN 9780520034143.

Frazer, Sir James George, *The Golden Bough: A Study in Magic and Religion*. 1890. New York, Macmillan, 1922.

Guerrier, Simon, *Bernice Summerfield: The Inside Story*. Maidenhead, Big Finish Productions Ltd, 2009. ISBN 9781844352807.

Hansen, Christopher J, ed, *Rumours, Peregrinations and Regenerations: A Critical Approach to Doctor Who*. Newcastle upon Tyne, Cambridge Scholars Publishing, 2010. ISBN 9781443820844.

Comer, Todd, 'Who Needs Family? I've Got the Whole World on My Shoulders: How the Doctor's Non-Domesticity Interrupts History'.

Hickman, Clayton, ed, *Doctor Who Annual 2006*. Tunbridge Wells, Panini Publishing Ltd, 2005. ISBN 9781904419730.

Hinnells, John R, *The Penguin Dictionary of Religions*. London, Penguin Books, 1984. ISBN 9780140511062.

Krockel, Carl, *War Trauma and English Modernism: TS Eliot and DH Lawrence*. New York, Palgrave Macmillan, 2011. ISBN 0230307752.

Langley, Travis, *Doctor Who Psychology: A Madman With a Box*. New York: Sterling Publishing, 2016. ISBN 9781454920014.

Erickson, Kristen, and Matt Munson, with Stephen Prescott and Travis Langley, 'Post-Time War Stress Disorder'.

Scarlet, Janina, and Alan Kistler, 'The Compassionate Doctor: Caring for Self by Caring for Others'.

Larsen, Stephen, and Robin Larsen, *Joseph Campbell: A Fire in the Mind – The Authorized Biography*. New York, Doubleday, 1991. ISBN 9780385266352.

McIntee, David A, *Sanctuary*. **Doctor Who: The New Adventures**. London, Virgin Publishing Ltd, 1995. ISBN 9780426204398.

Orchard, Andy, ed and trans, *The Elder Edda: A Book of Viking Lore*. London, Penguin, 2011. ISBN 9780140435856.

Parkin, Lance, and Lars Pearson, *Ahistory: An Unauthorised History of the Doctor Who Universe*. 3rd edition. Des Moines, Mad Norwegian Press, 2012. ISBN 9781935234111.

Peel, John, *Timewyrm: Genesys*. **Doctor Who: The New Adventures**. London, Virgin Publishing Ltd, 1991. ISBN 9780426203551.

Pratchett, Terry, *Hogfather*. London, Victor Gollancz, 1996. ISBN 9780575064034.

Purser-Hallard, Philip, *Dark Water / Death in Heaven*. **The Black Archive** #4. Edinburgh, Obverse Books, 2016. ISBN 9781909031401.

Snorri Sturlson, *The Prose Edda*. C 1220. Jesse L Byock, ed and trans, London, Penguin, 2005. ISBN 9780140447552.

Tokien, JRR, *The Lord of the Rings*. 1954-55. London, George Allen and Unwin, 1968. ISBN 9780048230874.

Vogler, Christopher, *The Writer's Journey: Mythic Structure for Storytellers and Screenwriters*. 1992. New revised edition, London, Boxtree Ltd, 1996. OSBN 9780752205571.

Periodicals

Doctor Who Magazine (DWM). Marvel UK, Panini, BBC, 1979-.

Abnett, Dan, *Pureblood*. DWM #193-196, cover dates November 1992 to February 1993.

Abnett, Dan, *Cuckoo*. DWM #208-10, cover dates January to March 1994.

Gray, Scott, *Ground Zero*. DWM #238-42, cover dates May to August 1996.

Jackson, Elizabeth, 'The 1996 *Doctor Who Magazine* Survey Results'. DWM #240, cover date July 1996.

Owen, Dave, 'The Best (and Worst) of Virgin'. DWM #265, cover date June 1998.

Television

Band of Brothers. DreamWorks, DreamWorks Television, HBO Films, 2001.

Doctor Who. BBC, 1963-.

Doctor Who Confidential. BBC, 2005-2011.

Alter Ego. 2007.

Firefly. Mutant Enemy Productions, 20th Century Fox Television, 2002.

Serenity, 2002.

Goodbye Mr Chips. BBC, 1984.

M*A*S*H. 20th Century Fox Television, 1972-83.

Heal Thyself, 1980.

Star Trek. Desilu Productions, Norway Corporation, Paramount Television, 1966-69.

The City on the Edge of Forever, 1967.

Mirror, Mirror, 1967.

Star Trek: The Next Generation. CBS Television Distribution, 1987-1994.

Encounter at Farpoint, 1987.

Haven 1987.

Second Chances, 1993.

To Serve Them All My Days. BBC, 1980-81.

Film

Anderson, Lindsay, dir, *If....* Memorial Enterprises, 1968.

Coppola, Francis Ford, dir, *Apocalypse Now.* United Artists, 1979.

Kubrick, Stanley, dir, *Full Metal Jacket.* Natant, Stanley Kubrick Productions, Warner Bros, 1987.

Lester, Richard, dir, *Superman II.* Dovemead Films, Film Export AG, International Film Production, 1980.

Lucas, George, dir, *Star Wars* (aka *Star Wars Episode IV: A New Hope*). Lucasfilm, Twentieth Century Fox Film Corporation, 1977.

McKay, Chris, dir, *The Lego Batman Movie*. DC Entertainment, Lego System A/S, Lin Pictures, 2017.

Scorsese, Martin, dir, *The Last Temptation of Christ*. Universal Pictures, Cineplex Odeon Films, 1988.

Audio CD

Cornell, Paul, and Mike Maddox, *Circular Time*. **Doctor Who**. Big Finish Productions, 2007.

Platt, Marc, *Spare Parts*. **Doctor Who**. Big Finish Productions, 2002.

Shearman, Rob, *Jubilee*. **Doctor Who**. Big Finish Productions, 2003.

Visual Art

Lea, Tom, *The 2,000 Yard Stare*. 1945.

Web

Archive of Our Own. http://archiveofourown.org. Accessed 12 March 2017.

Internet Movie Database. http://www.imdb.com/. Accessed 13 March 2017.

'Kate Orman'. Fanlore. https://fanlore.org/wiki/Kate_Orman. Accessed 12 March 2017.

'Poems and Poets of the First World War.' The Great War 1914-1918. http://www.greatwar.co.uk/poems/. Accessed 29 January 2017.

Binyon, Lawrence, 'For the Fallen'. http://www.greatwar.co.uk/poems/laurence-binyon-for-the-fallen.htm. Accessed 29 January 2017.

TV Tropes. http://tvtropes.org/. Accessed 2 May 2017.

'Doesn't Like Guns'. http://tvtropes.org/pmwiki/pmwiki.php/Main/DoesntLikeGuns. Accessed 12 March 2017.

'Thousand-Yard Stare'. http://tvtropes.org/pmwiki/pmwiki.php/Main/ThousandYardStare. Accessed 2 May 2017.

St Augustine, 'Homily 7 on the First Epistle of John'. New Advent. http://www.newadvent.org/fathers/170207.htm. Accessed 12 March 2017.

Bishop, David, 'A Conversation with Paul Cornell'. TSV #28. http://doctorwho.org.nz/archive/tsv28/paulcornell.html. Accessed 3 April 2017.

C, Lynn, 'Alternate Universes in Fan Fiction.' https://fanlore.org/wiki/Alternate_Universes_In_Fan_Fiction_(essay). Accessed 12 March 2017.

Cornell, Paul, *Human Nature*. Ebook edition. BBC **Doctor Who** website, 2002. Archived at the Wayback Machine Internet Archive. https://web.archive.org/web/20070707022110/http://www.bbc.co.uk/doctorwho/classic/ebooks/human_nature/index.shtml. Accessed 22 May 2017.

'Adapting the Novel for the Screen'.

Cornell, Paul, 'Paul Cornell: Novelist, Screenwriter, Comics Writer'. http://www.paulcornell.com/. Accessed 19 March 2017.

'Canonicity in Doctor Who'. http://www.paulcornell.com/2007/02/canonicity-in-doctor-who/. Accessed 19 March 2017.

'The Family of Blood'. http://www.paulcornell.com/2007/05/the-family-of-blood/. Accessed 19 March 2017.

Geoffrey of Monmouth. *The Life of Merlin* (*Vita Merlini*). John J Parry, trans, 1925. Internet Sacred Text Archive. http://www.sacred-texts.com/neu/eng/vm/index.htm. Accessed 15 April 2017.

Mills, Michael. '**Doctor Who** During the Wilderness Years'. On the Box, 10 May 2013. http://channelhopping.onthebox.com/2013/05/10/doctor-who-during-the-wilderness-years/. Accessed 29 January 2017.

Moffat, Steven, 'Blink: The Original Story'. BBC Doctor Who. http://www.bbc.co.uk/doctorwho/s4/features/stories/fiction_blink_the_original_story_01. Accessed 25 June 2017.

Mooney, Darren, 'Star Trek: The Next Generation – Imzadi by Peter David (Review)'. The m0vie blog, 2004. https://them0vieblog.com/2014/02/27/star-trek-the-next-generation-imzadi-by-peter-david-review/. Accessed 8 April 2017.

Morris, Mike, 'Adapt to Survive'. *The Doctor Who Ratings Guide*. http://pagefillers.com/dwrg/humanblood.htm. Accessed 3 May 2017.

Ortiz, Julio Angel, 'Throwback Interview: Paul Cornell (2002)'. Julio Angel Ortiz | Writer, 28 August 2014.

https://jaowriter.com/2014/08/28/throwback-interview-paul-cornell-2002/. Accessed 3 April 2017.

Scovell, Adam, 'Where to Begin with Folk Horror'. BFI. http://www.bfi.org.uk/news-opinion/news-bfi/features/where-begin-folk-horror. Accessed 18 January 2017.

Vogler, Christopher, 'A Practical Guide to Joseph Campbell's *The Hero with a Thousand Faces*'. http://www.thewritersjourney.com/hero's_journey.htm#Memo. Accessed 8 April 2017.

Williams, Owen, 'A History of British Folk Horror'. *Fangoria*, 18 October 2013. http://www.fangoria.com/new/a-history-of-british-folk-horror/. Accessed 6 March 2017.

BIOGRAPHIES

Naomi Jacobs is an academic whose research focusses on interaction, particularly in digital spaces, and with an emphasis on communities of media fans. She has written on how fans share and use 'gifs' and visual media, the digital footprint of fan conventions, and what zombie apocalypses might tell us about the spread of disease. She first became a fan of **Doctor Who** when, after watching the 1996 television movie and asking lots of questions, a friend told her 'There's these books by Virgin you should read...'

Philip Purser-Hallard is the series editor of **The Black Archive**, the editor of six science-fiction anthologies for Obverse Books, and the author of the **Devices** trilogy (*The Pendragon Protocol, The Locksley Exploit* and *Trojans*) and various novellas and short stories.